Linda Vannoy-Castillo ~~~~ ~~ ~~~ ~~~~ joy ~~~~~, uplifting
people I have ever met. When she walks into the room, hope and
encouragement walk in with her—and you walk out refreshed and a
whole lot lighter than when you walked in. I trust this will be your
experience as you read *Live without Borders*. Many people are at a
crossroads moment in their lives today. No matter their age, they
are at a point where they need more than a well-articulated theory.
What they need is truth that is rooted in a relationship with the
One who is the way, the life, and the truth. They need insights and
wisdom that are tried and true and have been learned experientially
on a journey with God and with like-minded, like-hearted others.
In the pages of *Live without Borders*, you will begin to believe there
is a new vision, purpose, and season for the life that is in front of
you. And you will receive the encouragement, hope, and wisdom
you need to live as fully as possible in God's redemptive purpose for
your life.

—MIKE BRADLEY, director, Alliance of Renewal Churches (ARC)

This book made me laugh and think. It is a must-read for any
Christian who needs a fresh perspective on life and God.

—JAMIE MANNING, author of *Thinking about Divorce*

This gal is a spitfire, and her heart is bigger than life! It all shows
through her humor and life experience as she spills it all out on the
pages of her book. I couldn't put it down. I laughed and cried at the
same time!

—AMY HONEY, author of *You Did Marry Prince Charming, You
Just Haven't Trained Him Yet*

I am so thankful God sent Linda Vannoy-Castillo to live and minister in the San Francisco Bay Area. Her eyes, her smile, and her story exude the love of Christ in a place that needs the gospel. This heartwarming book is about her story and how the transformation she experienced helps others discover their stories too.

—LINDA BERGQUIST, church planting catalyst and coauthor of *Church Turned Inside Out: A Guide for Designers, Refiners, and Re-Aligners* and *The Wholehearted Church Planter: Leadership from the Inside Out*

As I read *Live without Borders*, I enjoyed learning with Linda that "I am designed by God to do only what I can do." Linda reminds me that I am an original. Here are some teachings that the Holy Spirit highlighted for me through Linda's personal stories and experiences: There are adventures within the detours, especially the unplanned ones I encounter; remembering where I have been helps me to see where I am now and where I want to go tomorrow; and it's all about the journey, not the destination. I experienced what Linda prayed for me as a reader to happen: "You will laugh with me. You will cry with me. You will smile with me. And you will learn with me." Linda speaks from her heart about her journey on the road marked with joy and suffering. Enjoy the adventure with Linda.

—DR. JOE JOHNSON, founder and director of Heart of the Father Ministries, Laguna Woods, California

Live without Borders is a great book. I love it! God is love, and love is the most powerful force on earth—even in times of loss, love brings hope.

—BEATRIZ B. HERNANDEZ, author of *Down with Poverty: Manage Your Spending Habits without Compromising Your Needs–A Practical Guide to Finances of Bread Winners*

Everyone asks his or herself at some point in life, *Am I giving it everything I have? Am I letting my light shine as brightly as it can?* As a garden-variety pastor of a church for almost thirty years, I've been blessed to meet many people, and from the entire crowd, Linda Vannoy-Castillo is most likely to answer yes to both questions. Irenaeus (AD 130-202) once said that someone fully alive is the manifest glory of God. I invite you to dive into this book—the words of a woman fully alive. And may a little of the glory rub off on you.

—DAVID HOUSHOLDER, pastor, Robinwood Church, Orange County, California, and author of *The Blackberry Bush, Light Your Church on Fire Without Burning It Down*, and *The Seven Secrets of a Meaningful Life*

Linda Vannoy-Castillo's words are truly life-giving—not because every journey was a welcome one, but because God was with her on every one of those detours. For those seeking hope and healing, the lessons she shares can serve as a roadmap for navigating the difficult detours from which none of us are immune. For those experiencing grief, she provides an authentic witness to grieving well, which is often missing in our culture today. For those afraid to dream, whether for the first time or seemingly the thousandth time, Linda reminds us that God is always calling us to new adventures for our delight and for the sake of others. Get ready to have your life turned around!

—BILL AND LINDA WOODBURY, coauthors of *Enable-ism: Bridging the Recovery Gap Between the Family and the Addict*

Live without Borders

To my sweet, dear sister — Enjoy the MORE He has ahead
Sharyn

LINDA VANNOY-CASTILLO

lavish blessings

Linda

Joshua 1:7-9

BroadStreet
PUBLISHING

BroadStreet Publishing® Group, LLC
Savage, Minnesota, USA
BroadStreetPublishing.com

Live without Borders
Today Makes You Ready for Tomorrow.

978-1-4245-5761-5 (softcover)
978-1-4245-5762-2 (e-book)

Stock or custom editions of BroadStreet Publishing titles may be purchased in bulk for educational, business, ministry, fundraising, or sales promotional use. For information, please email info@ broadstreetpublishing.com.

Cover design by Chris Garborg at garborgdesign.com
Typesetting by Kjell Garborg at garborgdesign.com

Printed in the United States of America
18 19 20 21 22 5 4 3 2 1

This book is dedicated to my mom,

who gave birth to me—twice!

Contents

Foreword

When I was eighteen years old, I lived and breathed baseball. But as a boy growing up in northern Minnesota, I had to find unique ways to develop my skills. In the land of snow, ice, and hockey, serious baseball players are rare. As a sophomore in high school, I left my other athletic interests behind to focus solely on baseball. I began to train year-round. In the cold and dark of winter, I would get myself out of bed to train before school. I would train on vacation. Success on the baseball field began to consume me. I wanted no less than to become a Major League Baseball player.

The work and the dedication began to pay off. As a high school sophomore, junior, and senior, I was undefeated each year. I pitched every game allowed by our state rules, and I won every high school game I pitched for the Duluth Central Trojans. It wasn't a big stage, but my accomplishments and confidence were building to the point that I believed my Major League dream would likely come true.

For a select few, the cherry on top of a high school career is a chance to shine on a larger stage. When the Minnesota State High School League holds its annual, high school, all-star baseball game, it is the rare opportunity for high school seniors to showcase their playing abilities in front of hundreds of fans, coaches, college recruiters, and professional scouts.

I was chosen in the spring of 1995 to be the starting pitcher for one of two teams formed for the all-star game. I already had my scholarship to play baseball at Kansas State University and was now playing for a draft position in the Major League Baseball annual amateur draft the following month. With my scholarship secure, I had nothing to lose. Or so I thought.

As I prepared to take the field before the game, something happened. I threw a sizzling left-handed fastball to the catcher as hard as I could—straight into the ground in front of home plate.

Surprised by the sight, I threw another pitch. Same result. The ball that normally made a popping sound in the catcher's mitt now landed twenty feet in front of home plate. Again. And again. And again. And my stomach started to clench. I began to feel sick. And nervous. I didn't know why this was happening, but I was the starting pitcher and had to take the field to pitch to the best players in our state.

I took the field and began to warm up. And again, the ball bounced in front of home plate—every time. I couldn't seem to throw a pitch over the plate. The game was about to begin, and I was a nervous wreck.

What followed was the most difficult athletic performance of my life—or rather, unathletic performance. I couldn't throw a strike to save my life. I walked batters. I tried letting up on the speed to get it over the plate. When I did, they smashed the ball into the gaps. I hit my friend and future major leaguer in the foot.

By the time I walked off the field that day, I was an entirely different person. Needless to say, there wasn't a second inning for Matt Pfingsten. I was done for the day. But more than that, the unshakable confidence (arrogance, to be quite honest) that I had was gone. I was more than human. I was awful. I was embarrassing. And like it or not, my life was forever changed that day. My road had arrived at an intersection that I had not expected.

****

The road through life inevitably leads to pivotal crossroads when we realize that we are not in control. Our plans and expectations shatter. The life we had planned is no more, and this becomes painfully obvious. As we drive down the highway, it is the unexpected intersections that chart our true course. And as the author reminds us, we may not have a say in the intersections we face, but we do have a say in the direction we turn.

The book you are about to read is not like other books because the writer is not like other writers. Linda Vannoy-Castillo is one of the most inspiring people I've ever known. Her story of life, love, and loss is unlike anything you've ever heard. At times you will wonder if this can possibly be true. The answer is yes; it's all true. And she continues to walk through life today facing a new set of challenges you'll read about in the pages to come.

What sets Linda and this book apart is not only the

authenticity and genuineness of the story, but also Linda's heart as a pastor to make something beautiful of the challenges and tragedies she has faced in life. Her heart is not content to simply share an emotional, yet beautiful story with the reader and finish with the message that God is love. No. That's not the Linda I know. Linda walks the reader step by step through her own life to be a living example for us of how to learn from challenges and how to take practical steps to walk toward God in the midst of the most difficult seasons of life. Linda shows us so openly that if we examine her life of learning and growing with God, then we can see how God is working in our lives in ways that likely have never occurred to us.

Linda Vannoy-Castillo is a five-foot nothing, rainbow-haired Jesus-follower from the hills of San Francisco. If your road ever intersects with her in person, you will walk away inspired and moved to become closer to God in your walk with Him. I am personally inspired and moved by Linda's life. After reading this book, I have no doubt you'll feel the same.

God bless you,
Matt Pfingsten
President, Praying Pelican Missions

An Invitation

ADVENTURE

Adventurer: A person who enjoys or seeks
adventure (an unusual and exciting—
typically hazardous—experience or activity).

J do love a great adventure. Even a bad adventure is better
than no adventure at all. For, in fact, I am an adventurer.

I got my first small taste of adventure when I was seven—a
ride around the block on a motorcycle. I knew then that a life
lived large of doing new things was what I was truly made for.
I loved how free I felt—wind on my face and rushing through
my clothes. I felt no fear. Although I couldn't see anything in
front of me (except for the white T-shirt of my uncle's friend),
I wasn't afraid. I liked the speed (it was only later I learned that
he never got out of second gear!).

I loved the smells of the flowers and trees. I even loved the
smell of the bike, the tires, and the fumes. I loved the powerful

sound of the pipes. I loved being transported from point A to point B, wherever that landed me. Adventure was born in me on that summer afternoon!

And so began my thirst for more adventure—either through people or books. I learned to desire travel, movement, and new experiences—new places, foods, people, clothes, and environments. My daily life wasn't all that exciting, so I would escape into the lives of missionaries, artists, musicians, and friends. I would live vicariously through their adventures—even if it was just a visit to their grandma's house—dreaming it was me.

In those dreams, I was wearing colorful clothes, eating in places I had never been, and watching people move and speak. I was always laughing and aware of my surroundings and doing things that were both new and different. The intrigue of adventure drew me in, beckoning me to make it a regular part of my daily life.

I really had no fear, and I certainly didn't fear those unplanned or unexpected consequences that life tended to throw my way. Although I grew up to "fear" God, I was drawn to God more through love. I have always seen God as a God of adventure—One who had a plan for me—and that plan included a life full of new and often fun adventures. After all, every missionary I had read about left everything familiar. They ate new foods, traveled in new ways, learned new languages, and never did things the same way as they did in their familiar home environment. That sounded like plenty of adventure to me.

I didn't anticipate that a life of adventure serving God would be hard or challenging. It had to be fun and exciting, right? I've learned that the true spirit of adventure dwells not so much in the *where* but in the *how*. It is the *how* of "getting there" that is most important for me. As a Christ-follower, the same runs true for me in my spiritual life. My destination is sure (my home in heaven), but the journey God wants to take me on before I get there—well, that really matters to me, especially when I know God has planned the best adventure for me.

What adventure would you love to go on?

Where you want to go in life matters to God. He has made you with certain gifts, talents, and passions. He has placed these things in your life so that you can receive satisfaction and joy using those gifts. Yet, when given to God, they become supersized. They not only bless you, but they also bless and serve others. And when others are impacted—well, there's just no better feeling that comes from the deep satisfaction of seeing God work in others through you. It is like when you see the joy of watching someone open the gift you gave them for Christmas, and you see them jump in excitement or smile with deep joy when they realize that the very thing they wanted is the gift you have given.

God wants us to see that He has given us the best adventure—the one picked out just for us. Have you thought about going on the adventure of your life that includes real joy, deep happiness, and tons of surprises along the way? Go look, then come back. Let's go together.

1

Adventure Is Looking for You

THERE IS A PURPOSE AND A PLAN

> Life is either a daring adventure
> or nothing at all.
>
> *HELEN KELLER*

Although something lit within me that summer day when I enjoyed my first motorcycle ride, it would be ten years before the next opportunity for me to ride came during my freshmen year at Biola University in La Mirada, California. Again, a young man wearing a white T-shirt and jeans invited me on a Saturday ride with him through the local mountains surrounding the university. I was faced with a choice: accept the invitation or politely decline.

I immediately recalled my childhood memory with my uncle and readily accepted his invitation. I had no desire to drive the bike—sharing the ride as a passenger was fine with me. I was not concerned with the responsibilities of driving, navigating, and fueling in preparation of our ride. The only concern I had was to make sure I followed the instructions he had given me as to what clothes would be best to wear for my safety and comfort.

I knew that I would love the freedom of being away from my studies, schedules, and phone. And I was even more fortunate that he was really good looking. Seriously, I enjoyed the freedom of taking it all in—whatever "it" was. I had a wide-open mind and heart. No expectations—just the anticipation of gaining new input and experiences.

That day in early autumn, I was amazed as to what was happening within my soul. Inside, I felt like I was overflowing like a clear, bubbling spring. I can't explain it beyond the renewal that I sensed within me. That day ended too quickly, however. I never wanted to get off the bike, but my driver said we needed to do this every hour so that he could stretch and close down his mind for a few minutes.

I couldn't understand this at all as my perspective was totally different from his. I was busy looking around, smiling and laughing as we weaved through mountain roads. I had not realized the work it required of him to maneuver us through these same roads. I had been free to take in the smells of barbecues throughout the campsites and hear the squeals of kids splashing each other in little creeks. The sun was warming my body and made me feel connected to all of these sounds and smells.

Desire and passion were fanned like flames in my life that day. What a wonderful gift I had received from this young man, Terry, who would later become my husband. To be honest, I think I fell in love with riding before I fell in love with him. My desire and passion to take more rides, go on adventures, see things differently, and enjoy new experiences were born on the back of his motorcycle that day.

The truth is that God created us for desire and passion; He created us for adventure. We were created on purpose and for a purpose. We have been blessed with gifts and talents to do our job, love our friends and family, do what we could never imagine, and experience new things within and around us. God made us living creatures perfectly designed for abundant and full lives.

I began to understand why God gave us our senses. We get to experience a totality of life all around us as we see, hear, touch, taste, and feel. And not one experience is ever wasted. The people, pain, success, struggles (yes, the challenges too)— none of them are wasted.

God designed us to experience Him and His creation with full abandon, not just to stand back and observe what He has made. I began to feel so thankful and appreciative for all of His creation that autumn afternoon as I rediscovered the wonder my seven-year-old self had experienced first. It was a perfect moment to launch the rest of my adventures.

As an adult, I look back and realize there are some adventures in life I would *not* have chosen if there had been a clear detour on the road. Not all adventures are pleasant, thrill-seeking, or freeing. But there are certainly many adventures I have been privileged to experience and wish I could re-experience. Even the hardest adventures have shaped and molded me into who God has called me to be.

That first motorcycle ride with Terry was just the beginning of the thousands of miles throughout the United States and Canada we would cross and experience together. Each ride engaged our senses and gave us an appreciation for God's intentional designs for His children to enjoy.

Don't let what you *think* you cannot do discourage you from what you *can* do. Leading a life of adventure is a process that enriches your life and helps connect you to God's purpose for you. Living a life for God is a true adventure indeed!

NEW PERSPECTIVES

1. Acquire and listen to other life perspectives that may open doors to new experiences.

2. Search for new experiences that may reveal undiscovered desires and passions that bring joy into your life. Look up and consider the definitions of desire and passion as you search for these new experiences. What fuels desire and passion in you?

3. Don't be afraid of the challenges you face. The process of generating solutions to these challenges will stretch and shape you, and the abundance of challenges you face enable you to live a full life.

4. Invite God to design your day. He has intention for you each and every day. Read Jeremiah 29:11 and be encouraged to know that God has a purpose and plan for your life.

2

Choosing Your Driver

MAKING WISE CHOICES

Oh, the joys of those who trust the LORD ...
O LORD my God, you have performed many
wonders for us. Your plans for us are too
numerous to list.

PSALM 40:4–5

*H*ave you ever noticed that when friends and relatives embark on a trip—even to the shopping mall or grocery store, the first question that follows the decision of the destination is, "Who's driving?" This question often becomes all the more important when the potential drivers include a young or new driver. People automatically become discerning of that person's experience and skill, regardless of the distance.

This same discernment rings especially true when driving

a motorcycle. Whenever you are the rider or passenger, like I was on that first ride with Terry, it is imperative that you trust the experience of the person you are sitting behind.

Although I had the passion and the desire to experience the world from the back of a motorcycle, I found that I became pretty picky about who would accompany me on my adventures. I began to ask Terry about his experiences on a bike. He had to field my questions, concerns, and excitement. Questions like:

- How long have you been driving a motorcycle?
- Did you have any training on this particular bike?
- Do you have a valid license?
- Have you ever been in an accident?
- How often do you take passengers on your bike?
- In the event of a mechanical problem, can you fix it?
- Do you follow the law and obey road signs?
- How fast do you normally drive?

I needed to know more about his leadership, his self-control, his ability to anticipate problems, and whether or not he was likely to take unnecessary risks—especially with me as his passenger. It was my job to be informed and shrewd in my assessment of his answers. Only then could I decide if I was willing to entrust my life to him on his bike. I wanted to be smart. I needed to know, and I realized this was a big decision for me.

As I thought and prayed regarding my decision, I found myself praying for Terry. He would need wisdom on the road as he often had to make quick decisions. His bike would need mechanical attention. Both of us would need to remain alert in order to protect ourselves from other drivers and road hazards.

God heard each of my prayers. In all those years and between all those miles on various bikes, I am thankful we never broke down (although we came close). We never ran out of gas (although fumes once carried us to a gas station in the nick of time). We never had an accident.

I knew my driver loved me and treated me well by addressing my questions, apprehensions, and short-term fears. While I was on a bike with Terry, he had complete control of my life, and he drove like I was his precious cargo. I can honestly say that I never had any fear when I rode with Terry. He liked to travel all day; I loved that best about him. I saw some gorgeous sunrises and sunsets because we never seemed able to get enough riding into a single day.

Just like on the road, in life we face countless decisions that determine our paths. We answer questions like: *What do you want to be when you grow up? Do you want to get married? What type of person do you want to marry? Do you attend church? Which one? What activities do you enjoy? What kind of friends do you hang out with?* The answers to these questions determine the direction of your life: where you receive your education, where you live, who you trust, and ultimately who you share your adventures in life with.

How many people would you trust with 100 percent

confidence with your life? I am glad that when I checked out God's credentials and His desire to share adventure with me, He always passed with flying colors. He has shown His care for me and all my questions, apprehensions, and short-term fears in life that He is deserving of my trust, faith, and dependence on Him.

God doesn't take unnecessary risks with us. In fact, He always has our best path in mind. You must have complete and total faith and trust in the people with whom you share your life adventure. They must be people you can depend on—friends who will be with you during the good times and the hard times. Friendship takes us by the hand and reminds us that we are not alone on our journeys.

You can choose God today to assist you in your decision-making and even meeting the friends who will come alongside your adventure. He has the best adventure ahead for you! You are not done yet!

NEW PERSPECTIVES

1. Be prepared to make choices. Smart choices will help keep you focused on the things you want to accomplish in life.
2. Be inquisitive. Never be afraid to ask questions and seek answers.
3. Choose your friends wisely as you consider your destiny.
4. Surround yourself with people who truly care about you, love you, and only want the best for you!

5. Reread Jeremiah 29:11 and Psalm 40:4–5 and know that God has the best plans in store for you. If you can't see them yet, spend time praying through your questions, concerns, and fears, and trust God to see you safely through each adventure.

3

Getting the Bike and Yourself Ready

TODAY MAKES US READY FOR TOMORROW

By failing to prepare, you are preparing to fail.

BENJAMIN FRANKLIN

Preparation is essential for an adventurous ride, and a considerable amount of planning and work must be done beforehand. You need to:

- select your final destination,
- plot your primary route of travel (and backup routes),
- scout weather conditions,
- ensure your gear is well-maintained and ready for use,
- stow an assortment of tools on the bike (you never know what you might need!),

- conduct routine bike maintenance, such as checking fluid levels and tire pressure, and
- anticipate the unknown.

Bike maintenance is especially important because it's impossible to have an adventure if the motorcycle isn't functioning. Be sure you continually perform routine maintenance on your bike so you're familiar with the sounds and rhythms of a well-running machine. If you're attuned to your bike, you'll learn to recognize subtle abnormalities that may indicate a problem. And if there's a problem you can't fix, it's time to take it to a professional.

God has a plan for all of us—including seasons of preparation. Sometimes, the preparation takes so long that we end up changing our minds and hearts about pursuing a dream or adventure. These delays allow us to consider the costs involved in our pursuit, and although they may be frustrating, delays are one of the greatest gifts we can receive. Throughout the road of life, it's important to frequently reassess whether that dream or adventure is something we want to keep pursuing. Once the delay is resolved, the feelings of passion and motivation well up again and propel you forward.

While a bike needs regular maintenance, our lives need regular maintenance as well—health check-ups, vacations, short pick-me-ups, encouragement from others, and challenges to others. Our relationship with Jesus requires routine maintenance. The Bible says in John 10:27 that we should know the sound of Jesus' voice, and we must stay close to Him so that it's familiar to us. Jesus knows how to fix whatever may be wrong in our lives through His Word, His accessibility to us through prayer, and His people who surround us. This routine life maintenance allows us to make small adjustments whenever the sounds of our lives start to squeak, sputter, or scream for attention.

Fine-tuning and adjusting my life was a mind-set placed within me at the age of five. My mom, having been raised Roman Catholic, made a spiritual life change. As the oldest daughter in her family, she carried the expectations of her parents to succeed in all areas of her life—including her spiritual life. Mom practiced Catholicism as closely as expected, but some of the answers to her questions and some of the Catholic practices didn't satisfy her soul.

Growing up, my mom was taught that she had to confess her sins to a priest, who would then prescribe acts of contrition for her to perform in order to receive forgiveness for her sins. Searching for answers, she found herself in attendance at a Billy Graham Crusade in San Francisco. That evening, she was introduced to Christ as her personal Savior—the One who would walk with her in a direct relationship and without the intervention of another person. She was thrilled that God Himself would forgive her sins. She loved that she was a daughter of the King Most High, and that she could go directly to Him with her confessions and concerns.

That night in San Francisco began my mom's lifelong love affair with God and her insatiable desire for His Word. She began to share this good news with my younger brother and me at every opportunity. As I look back, I can see clearly how she was preparing us with the two best tools we could have for a life of adventure: a relationship with God and a love for His Word.

My relationship with God began on a foggy summer day in July shortly after Mom's life-changing experience in San Francisco. It had been a tough morning for my mom. I was acting up, and I had frustrated her so much that she sent me outside to think about what I had done. As soon as I was sent outside, I immediately went looking for a way back into the house—only to find she had locked the doors to secure a few peaceful minutes to herself. She even locked the windows and drew the curtains (yep, I had really upset her).

Outside was cold and damp, and I didn't like being stuck out there. In my persistence to get inside, I discovered that the kitchen window was still open a little bit. It was above our kitchen sink and too high for me to climb through, so I decided to do the next best thing my young mind could think of: I began to sing every single song I had learned in Sunday school at the top of my lungs. It wasn't long before my mom peeked through the window and asked me to come back inside before the neighbors called to complain. My plan had worked, and I was back inside!

My mom invited me to sit beside her at the kitchen table where her black, leather Bible laid open. She read Scripture to me and helped me follow along as her finger touched each word. I can still hear her voice as she read: "Look! I stand at the door and knock. If you hear my voice and open the door, I will come in, and we will share a meal together as friends" (Revelation 3:20).

She told me that Jesus stands at the door of my heart and knocks, and He wants to come into every part of my life. I looked down at my blouse, and she quickly clarified that the passage didn't mean my physical heart, but the part of me that thinks about doing good things or bad things. I recalled how I had acted toward her earlier in the day, and her words hit home. She went on to explain that I choose whether I let Him into my heart, and that Jesus is a gentleman who would never force Himself inside. I remember her showing me an old painting that depicted Jesus knocking on the door of a home within a forest. She pointed out that the door lacked a doorknob or handle for Jesus to use because He knocks and waits for someone to open the door.

It was people's choices to do bad things, she explained, that made Jesus leave heaven to live on earth. I learned that day how my sins separated me from God, but because He loved me so much, Jesus took my place on the cross and paid for all of humanity's sins—including mine, so that when I died, I could live in heaven with Jesus and God forever. Even better than that, she told me Jesus offered to come into my life right then, and we could enjoy life together—like having meals together as a family; I liked that visual. I also liked the idea of someone who would live with me forever, so I would never be alone!

My mom then asked me if I would like to invite Jesus into my life, and I responded with an enthusiastic, "Yes!" She took my hand and led me into her bedroom. We knelt down on the floor next to the bed, and I repeated a prayer after her. In that prayer, I told Jesus I was sorry for the bad things I had done, and that I was opening the door of my heart to invite Him inside. I felt clean and at peace. My mom hugged me, beaming. I asked her if I could have a Bible of my own with my name engraved on it, like hers. She thought for a moment.

"Oh, Linda," she said smiling, "that would be wonderful for you to have one, but we will have to wait until your birthday."

I asked how far away it was and felt discouraged when she told me my birthday was almost one hundred days away. My "boo-boo" face appeared as I pushed out my lower lip. But then she added another condition that made me even more unhappy.

"I will gladly give you that Bible with gold letters spelling your name for your birthday," she told me, "but you will need to memorize fifty verses."

"*Fifty* verses?" I exclaimed. "I'm only five years old," I quickly reminded her, hoping to turn the tide in my favor.

"Linda, I know you can do this," my mom reassured me. "You know some verses already, and you can ask your Sunday school teacher to help you too."

I embraced the challenge and received my first Bible with my very own name engraved in gold letters on the cover when

I was six years old. That challenge turned out to be the beginning of many Scripture memorization challenges. I earned my next Bible, a pretty pink one, when I was eight by memorizing another 150 verses. By the time I was twelve, I had earned a dark blue Bible for memorizing another 250 verses and for reading the entire Bible in a year (something I've done every year since). Then, as I prepared to enter high school and had plans to attend a Christian university, my mom brought the largest challenge yet: She asked me to memorize five hundred new verses every year of high school (a total of two thousand verses) to receive my new Bible for college. I began to memorize entire chapters and portions of books of the Bible.

The amazing thing about all of this memorization is that God doesn't let any of the passages we deposit into our hearts, souls, and minds go to waste. Truly, God's Word is the only thing I know in my life to be absolutely true. His Word is about truth, goodness, discipline, promises, and justice; it is the same yesterday, today, and forever. I have continued to learn more about God and His character as I learn and memorize more of His Word. He has always been by my side. True to His promise, He has eaten every meal with me and continues to walk through life beside me—never leaving me even in my hardest of times, even when He has seemed distant.

God waits for all of us to invite Him into our lives. He is faithful to our needs as we are faithful to His Word. I have tried to live by His Words—not always successfully—but I know He won't push me away when I return to Him. His love and

His grace are that lavish! God is near in the fun, celebratory times in our lives, and He is also close when we are broken-hearted. The tools my mom gave me by teaching me how to have a personal relationship with Christ and the importance of reading, knowing, and memorizing God's Word have served as necessary preparation for what I would face in my life. I am thankful for her influence and guidance.

NEW PERSPECTIVES

1. Attend to the routine maintenance of your life. Perform checkups on your emotional, psychological, and physical states, and remember that vacations and regular rest are equally important as work.
2. Pay attention to what you're thinking. Evaluate the input you're receiving from your eyes, ears, and heart. All of it helps prepare you to make decisions.
3. What we consider to be truth ultimately guides us. Whose words do you consider to be truth?

4

Reading a Map

DIRECTION IS IMPORTANT IN OUR LIVES

The LORD says, "I will guide you along the best
pathway for your life. I will advise you and
watch over you."

PSALM 32:8

The first step to any great adventure is to decide your direction, destination, and distance. Where do you want to go today? Then determine your time commitment: How much time do you want to devote to this particular adventure? Identify the anticipated terrain and road conditions (i.e., mountains, deserts, etc.) and collect information about the area—be it through personal experience or the experiences of others. Consider any challenges the weather may pose and what kind of gear will be most appropriate. To properly complete your planning, you'll need maps: paper maps, internet resources, or a phone application.

Once you've obtained your maps, you'll have to mark your destination and note alternate routes, as well as any metropolitan or rural communities you're likely to pass through. You'll also want to be aware of the traffic conditions you may encounter, the rest stops where you intend to rest, and the gas stations, food, and stores where you can stock up on supplies. Personally, I enjoy looking for alternate routes to bring me home. I often plan one route to the destination and a different route back home. I hate repeating cement because I like to see and experience other communities.

A paper map, however, doesn't warn you of road conditions or closures. The best tool for that type of information is a global positioning system (GPS), which will even show where any gnarly traffic may be. Maps provide elevation information and mile markers between each city, while GPS gets you from one point to the next on the most efficient route. Some maps (especially gas station maps) will show their company's gas emblem to indicate stations along your route; GPS will do that for you if you take the time to request it periodically along your drive.

Both paper maps and GPS are great to have, but even with these tools you may still experience delays and wonder whether you'll ever arrive at your destination. Paper maps have their limitations and frustrations. Take it from me: As a missionary, I have both professional and personal travel experience. I have journeyed through mountains and cities equipped with only a detailed map, which hardly seemed to help.

On one ride, Terry and I drove in circles—then bigger circles—looking for our next turn, which was supposed to be on Sixtieth Street. We hadn't anticipated the extra miles from getting lost, and I anxiously kept checking the fuel gauge. We stopped several times to ask locals for directions, but the language barrier seemed insurmountable; we couldn't seem to effectively communicate with anyone. We were driving down one-ways in the wrong direction; drivers were honking their horns at us, and the language, tone, and volume between Terry and me was becoming toxic. On top of all that, a monsoon-type rainfall started pouring down from the skies. The flash-flood conditions forced us to pull into a parking lot and reconsider our options.

We couldn't help each other, and we had no one to call or ask for help or directions. Frustrated to the point of tears, we considered driving back home. The stress of being lost was too much, and it was robbing us of our joy. We eventually realized that the Sixtieth Street we were in search of was just one of four streets also named Sixtieth Street in that very same city. Of course, we traveled to each Sixtieth Street before finally turning down the right one.

It wasn't until many days later that we realized the storm probably saved our adventure; it certainly saved our sanity and redeemed our interactions with each other. Had we not pulled into a parking lot to take a deep breath and release the tension in our bodies, we may have never found Sixtieth Street. Doesn't that sound a lot like life at times?

Traveling with a GPS is filled with its own set of challenges. In the summer of 2014, I was serving in Puerto Rico for a few months as a missionary with Praying Pelican Missions. It became clear to me that summer that I have a very different way of navigating than Kristina (the name I'd given the voice of my GPS). I first learned to navigate with a paper map, so I like to read the numbers for highways rather than their regional names. For me, numbers are easier to identify quickly while driving or riding. Kristina, however, prefers to read the names. Our differences came to a head every time I approached a junction. She would tell me the name of a road to turn onto, but only signs with numbers stared back at me. After a few weeks of (many) mistakes and poor decisions, I eventually learned how to properly use the map on my GPS.

Our relationship was rocky at first, but Kristina was helpful. She wisely prepared me for the next turn with reminders at a mile, and then a quarter mile, and again when the time came to turn. I actually learned some faith skills from Kristina. When I was unsure whether to turn, or if the street signs I read didn't match the street name she spoke, all was good as long as I turned when she directed. Kristina proved quite handy whenever I happened to make a wrong turn, as she would quickly recalculate and determine the best route from there.

So often in life we lose sight of where we are going and

how we are getting there. We have to adjust and redirect to get back on track. We may also find ourselves in need of new resources and fresh wisdom to make those adjustments, so that we can keep our focus on what is truly important to us and our future. Sometimes we experience an event of enormous consequence that shifts our perspective. Then there are times when our lives are altered by circumstances, through no fault of our own, and it affects us emotionally, spiritually, and mentally. Even with unexpected new paths, we learn to recover from distress and disappointment, and we begin to continue life's adventures. Even those moments of downpour can become a period of rest and reflection.

Just as it's impossible to set out on a successful motorcycle adventure without preparation, it's also impossible to fulfill your vision for your life or your dream without asking yourself some important questions. You have to consider the direction you want to go in, the tools you will need, and the resources you'll require. Do you need to go back to school? Can you accomplish that vision or dream where you are, or will you need to move elsewhere? Who has already been where you want to go? Can they offer insight or information? Get these conversations going! Find out! What is your vision for the end of this journey? Are you a sightseer or an explorer?

The mind-set of a sightseer is very different from that of a committed adventurer or explorer. Sightseers arrive at their destinations to simply take in the landscape; they're unsure of what they may learn or accomplish by the end of their trip.

Explorers, on the other hand, spend a lot of time meticulously planning and preparing for their journey and the goal they seek to accomplish.

In order to successfully achieve your vision, you need to keep the final destination in mind at all times—while you fuel up, while you ask for directions, while you stop and take a moment to be awed by everything that's around you. You have faced frustrations that had you ready to quit; celebrate how far you've come and be encouraged by your strength. Or perhaps it's time to go home, reassess, readjust, and change into your rain gear for the storms ahead.

During times of frustration (with or without Kristina or a map), I always go back to the analogy of God as my driver—the one who guides me and whose presence I desire while I travel. I love that the Lord has all of us on different journeys. We meet each other along the way: those who are ahead of us, those who are beside us, and those who are behind us. The journey is about the process; perfection is not the goal. Some of the most delicious food, gorgeous landscapes, and wonderful people I have experienced have happened when I've been lost. Don't get me wrong, I do not like to be lost or delayed, but I've learned that wrong turns often lead to great memories. Our struggles provide opportunities for growth in ways that times of comfort can't replicate. Difficulties are to be expected; they help prepare us for the changes ahead.

Please know that our God never wastes anything—not even poor choices. We know there are consequences to those choices, but God has a miraculous way of redeeming them. He offers profound grace and mercy and showers us with things we don't deserve. As a loving Father and guide who is our strength, hope, hiding place, and intercessor, He gives and gives—never taking His gaze from us. He desires for us to enjoy the best of all things and sometimes that's going to include tough, hard work. In fact, He gives us all the tools, wisdom, guidance, and resources we will need to be everything He dreams for us.

Look around you! Grab your stuff! You are going on an adventure right now! The psalmist said, "For you are my hiding place; you protect me from trouble. You surround me with songs of victory. The LORD says, 'I will guide you along the best pathway for your life. I will advise you and watch over you'" (Psalm 32:7–8).

NEW PERSPECTIVES

1. Ask yourself where you want to be in the next month, next year, and in five years. Write your answers down and then begin to plan what you will need to do to accomplish that vision.

2. Create categories for your vision for your life, such as family, relationships, career, health, hobbies, and travel. Then list your answers from number one under the appropriate categories. Organizing your goals will help you prioritize them and lead you to investigate the relevant training and resources you may need to obtain.

3. Tell someone your goals.
4. Celebrate your progress and your accomplishments monthly.

5

Clothes Make the Ride

WHAT SURROUNDS US MATTERS

You have clothed him with splendor
and majesty. You have endowed him
with eternal blessings and given him
the joy of your presence.

PSALM 21: 5–6

When I get ready to go on any adventure—whether it's for vacation or work—it is important to dress properly and protect myself from the elements. Maybe you are like me when preparing for a trip, checking the weather forecast and tripping over suitcases and clothing strewn all about the bed and floor. The challenge is to avoid overpacking while also preparing yourself for any possible changes in weather. Regardless of your destination, some essentials must always be packed. On every motorcycle trip, essentials include a leather jacket, leather pants, gloves, and a helmet. Essential accessories include a face guard, extra clothing, socks, and rain gear.

One of my favorite, must-see, must-shop (hopefully) locations is a Harley Davidson dealership. It's always fun to see and meet the people in these stores. I love how each store sells clothes with designs of their local city on them. Be it hot or cold on the road, I can buy apparel I look good in. My excitement for the Harley Davidson dealerships also makes me wonder about what's important to me. Is it comfort? Travel? Vacations? Positive as opposed to negative people? Entertainment? Social interactions? God tells us in Ephesians 6 to protect ourselves and put on clothing for the battles and challenges in our lives. Some essentials must be protected—like our minds, hearts, and families, and we also need to protect our accessories, like our gifts, possessions, and talents.

Terry was one of those essential pieces in my life. He reintroduced me to the idea that life is an adventure—one that should be respected, desired, and experienced, and he introduced me to seeing the urban and rural landscape differently. Rather than using streets, Terry preferred to drive in alleys and on dirt roads. He would avoid congested traffic lanes and drive around the hills of a neighborhood to view a sunrise or a sunset. We created roads where there weren't any before.

He introduced me to the safety of sharing secrets without judgment. We'd arrive at one of our destinations, which was usually wherever we were when the engine shut off. This feeling of safety developed into trusting, liking, respecting, and then loving him. He showed me what it would be like to receive the safety, trust, respect, and love of this man—and he promised to love me forever. Best of all, he would love me even when I was less than loveable and acting like a brat. He said he would never go away, and he promised that I wouldn't die alone.

Now that I'm an older adult, I know that no one can guarantee those kinds of promises. But that didn't stop us from expressing our hearts and making promises to each other back then. We dreamed about our future. We dreamed about how we would live our life together in such a way that we would make a difference; we would try to impact the lives of everyone we met. We dreamed about us.

My freshman year of college was wonderful because Terry was in it. We shared the struggles of being students, of finding time for one another, and of having little money. We found that buying gasoline for his motorcycle served as a kind of protective clothing for our relationship: with it, we could weather any storm together and still have fun along the way.

The summer between our freshman and sophomore years brought a new set of challenges. Terry was accepted into the US Army and had to report to boot camp at Fort Ord, California in October. This would change everything—our times together, our rides together, and our dreams together. We took on the challenge, confident we could see this adventure through.

I traveled up to Northern California with his mom and grandma in a huge automobile—a late 1960s Cadillac that could probably fit a zillion people. The three of us ladies chatted Terry's ear off the entire eight-hour drive. Once we arrived, we found lodging and ate dinner together. Terry and I watched the sunset and talked all night in each other's arms on the patio of his mom's and grandmother's suite. We all ate breakfast early and then took him to report to boot camp. And just like that, he was gone.

The following year was filled with short phone calls, long love letters, and countless visits to the post office to mail home-made cookies. I had an awesome year of college and enjoyed the person emerging within me. Terry finally graduated from boot camp and completed an additional school in Texas. We couldn't wait to share longer conversations and have more opportunities to speak of our love in each other's presence that summer before my junior year. Even though we had spent a year apart, our love was still so alive, and we knew we were blessed. Although I was living at home in the San Francisco Bay Area during the summer, he visited whenever he could, and we recognized the special gift we had in our relationship.

When I arrived at Biola University over Labor Day week-end, Terry picked me up on the motorcycle. I was so thrilled to experience the freedom of being away from every care in the world again and recalled how our relationship began on that bike. He took me to the same place we had stopped on our very first ride together—oh, was I smiling big now! You know it's true romance when a man remembers seemingly insignificant moments and details from a relationship. He dropped to his knee and pulled out a small box. My smile grew even larger, and my eyes began to leak. He opened the box to reveal a beautiful ring and said, "Will you become my bride and my wife for all of our lives forever?" Before I could answer, he said, "I already asked your stepdad, and he said I could take your hand after you finish college, and after I'm done with my service to the army." I fell to my knees and smothered him with kisses and tears. This was truly the best day of my life, and I just knew many more adventures were to come.

Then the following month, Terry received orders to ship to Vietnam for a year. Thankfully, this was toward the end of this long-fought conflict, but his job as a medic would be dangerous. He would be flying dust-off, which meant he would pick up every dead or injured man on the battlefield and return them to the military base.

We cried, we prayed, and we held one another. I called home for some advice. My mom suggested I return the ring before I became a young widow and wait for him to return while I continued my education. I didn't know how I would break the news to Terry. Before he deployed, I suggested to him that we go back to "our place" where we got engaged. In the conversation that followed, he promised that I would always have his heart, and he would find me again if his orders would take him beyond his initial orders to Vietnam. I held him, took the ring off of my finger, and handed it to him.

I explained that I had to listen to older, wiser advice, but I would pray for the day of his return because he promised to find me again. It was one of the hardest days of my life, and my heart hurt long after it.

I returned to Biola and immersed myself in my studies, which reminded me of my desire and purpose for coming to this university. The focus helped my heart heal. I became active in missions—both domestically and internationally, and I assisted local outreach events both on and off campus. After graduation, I became a missionary in Argentina where I assisted kids who were living in a boarding school while their parents served as full-time missionaries. My job was to help these kids receive an education, so that they could later transition into American educational environments when they were older. I also assisted the local churches with their children's outreach programs.

While I was appreciative of the letters and calls from home, I learned the importance of serving God alone. My heart at times remembered the promise Terry made to me years before, but so far he had not found me. I realized I had never visited his grandmother's or mom's home to look for him. I didn't think it would be proper or right for me to do the looking, but my heart still watched for him.

God was with me on an overcast afternoon in Argentina when a doctor told me I had cervical cancer. I was twenty-three years old. My head swirled; my thoughts were as cloudy as the weather outside. All I wanted to do was run out the door and call my mom. Thankfully, I had other missionaries around me to hold me, wipe my tears, and calm me down before I made the call to my mom to tell her I was coming home. I would need further treatment and observation stateside.

I needed to be alone with God to sort through all of the varying emotions. I had tough questions to face. My entire life had been singularly focused on accepting the call to missions. I dreamed about it and read every biography and autobiography about missionaries I could get my hands on. I had written to missionaries all over the world who I didn't know well but who kindly answered all of my questions. I was living overseas and serving others. I had prepared carefully and thoughtfully for this life, so why would God change His mind and send me back home? Where was my purpose? What was I going to do now? Was cancer going to kill me (and my dream)? What if I couldn't return here? Where was my hope? And if the rules were now changed—well, I was disappointed with God.

And the rules did change. I flew home to the States and have yet to return to Argentina. I was disappointed. I loved the people, the ministry, the food, and the deep satisfaction from the work I was doing for God. The plan was for me to endure all the doctor visits and procedures back home and then wait through that first year to see if anything else developed. Once I received a clean bill of health, I could return to Argentina.

However, as my one-year date neared, another test showed that I had uterine cancer. The treatment would require a surgery that would leave me unable to have my own children. I watched in despair as I saw the door to dream number two swing to a close before my eyes.

Oh God, I prayed, *help me see you in all of these things. Right now I am afraid to dream or want anything. I know deep down that you see me, and that you have always had a purpose for my life. I thought ... I just thought ... I would have an ordinary life. I never imagined it would be this hard.*

The questions and emotions that we face in the challenging moments of life (both the good and the bad) often startle us with the realities of what we must face. These feelings swing us back and forth on a pendulum between sorrow and joy—both part of life's adventure.

After I had returned to the States for my treatment, my mom invited me to come alongside my parents' ministry and work with the children's program. We also started a day camp for working parents in need of great care for their kids. I always knew God called me to serve in ministry with kids on the mission field. Location never mattered, so why not serve in the streets of cities within the United States? As the Southern California director, I ministered alongside churches to help them recruit volunteers, assist them in their vision, train their volunteers, and train their leaders to lead missionary trips domestically and internationally.

In the middle of this exciting time in my life came an adventure within an adventure: life in the midst of cancer treatments—with all the side effects, reactions, and exhaustion. I have found that when your heart is hurting, and you're struggling to cope each day, your perspective on life begins to skew; it becomes ambiguous. My dreams of marriage and family were all but dead. I struggled with my self-confidence. The chemotherapy and radiation had left me bald, tired, and convinced that no potential suitor would find me attractive. Having embraced that mind-set, you can imagine the shock I felt when I found myself in a surprise reunion with Terry on my thirty-fifth birthday.

My birthday dawned, and I had a doctor appointment and ministry commitments in a nearby city. Afterward, I had plans to meet up with a friend from college for the evening. I was grateful for the chance to be out on my birthday, as I knew few people in the area. We were enjoying a quick bite at a restaurant before attending a movie, and I noticed a gentleman sitting a few tables over with four ladies, each one of them laughing. We kept catching each other's eye and locking our gaze. Those sparkly blue eyes, dark hair, and high cheekbones seemed familiar, but I just couldn't put the pieces together. I didn't even recognize Terry at first, and later I found out he had also been trying to remember my name. Clearly we had both changed a lot. I was certainly not the same woman he had known. I was bald from cancer treatments and certainly not as feisty as I had been when we were younger.

Terry's friend, who had been sitting at that table as well, later told me Terry had remarked, "Hey, I think I know that woman sitting at the table over there."

"Really, Terry?" they asked, "Who is she?"

"That's the thing. If it's who I think it is, we were engaged once," he answered, still trying to put the pieces together himself.

"Seriously, Terry?" they responded in surprise, "We didn't know you were engaged before. That's so cool! You need to get over there. They look like they're about to leave."

"Oh, I can't do that," he said. "I don't even remember her name." (Seriously, we laughed about this later because what happened next is even more amazing.)

Again, his friends encouraged him to talk to me. They told him he had nothing to lose, and the "I-think-we-were-engaged-at-one-time" line was a good opener. They helped him script the line and told him to end with, "Is it true? What is your name? Let's figure out this mystery."

Terry left his table and came over to mine. My friend and I stood up to leave, but I saw him walking toward me, so I took my time, hoping we would have a chance to talk. He stood next me and said, "Linda?" I could hear the hopeful anticipation in his voice.

"Terry?" I asked.

We realized how remarkable and miraculous the words we spoke really were once we learned each other's backstory. The profound, lavish love of God was poured out on me in that walk across a restaurant. God was clothing me in His profound attention to my heart, especially at such a low time in my life.

Terry and I decided to meet for lunch the next day and, after some directions, we went our separate ways. Throughout the entire movie I tried to figure out a way to ditch my friend and return to the restaurant. I later found out Terry hadn't stayed at the restaurant for long. He told his coworkers he needed to buy a new outfit because his life was about to change. He was focused on clothing himself properly for our meeting the following day.

I barely slept that night and instead wondered what the day would bring. I thanked God for this second chance. We embraced the next day when we met, and tears shone in both of our eyes. We knew this was a wonderful gift, and when we held hands later that day, well, it was as if no time had passed at all.

Our God wants to meet the desires of our hearts, even the ones we don't speak aloud. How thankful I continue to be for the gift of friendship that clothes us when we feel we are unworthy or not good enough or pretty enough or smart enough. He has clothes picked out for us that come in the forms of friendship, family, and love. His presence tells us that we are worthy of His love, and He has created us to reflect Him. Surround yourself with His words and the gifts of supportive people in your life.

NEW PERSPECTIVES

1. Cultivate healthy relationships around you.
2. Surround yourself with three kinds of people:
   - Those who are ahead of you in life, so that you may learn from them.

- Those who are behind you, so that you may help and empower them.
- Those who are beside you to lift you up, celebrate your wins with you, and help you process losses and challenges.
3. Look and seek for the God who loves you, who sacrificed Himself for you, and who promises to never desert you.

6

Road Signs Matter

GUIDANCE IS ALWAYS NEARBY

Whether you turn to the right or to the left,
your ears will hear a voice behind you, saying,
"This is the way; walk in it."

ISAIAH 30:21

What kind of road signs catch your eye? Some signs alert you to lower your speed due to local traffic laws, construction, or road conditions. Others warn you of potential road hazards. Whether these signs bring good news or delays, their words prepare you for the road ahead, so be sure to pay attention to them.

Has a friend, pastor, doctor, or family member ever shared words of preparation with you? Have you ever heard their words and later realized they helped prepare you for something that was to come? Some signs are only illustrations without any words. These illustrated signs can be especially tricky if you are in an unfamiliar region or country, and that's where the experience of others is particularly helpful.

Listen to those who have traveled ahead of you. They've been where you are, and they can draw a picture of what you may experience as you journey on. A road map from someone who has traveled the same route could save you tons of grief, money, heartache, and sleep. Finding these dear individuals who are willing to walk alongside you and share portions of their life with you is invaluable!

After an absence of fifteen years, reconnecting with Terry and holding his hand that next day certainly felt like a sign that we would finally be together. But could that be the case? Were we reading the signs correctly? Everything about us had changed. Was it even possible for us to begin to share a life together after we had each taken such sharp and different turns in our lives? I was facing treatment and surgery the following week. Would Terry walk with me on this journey I had found myself on?

In my mind, I changed his name from Terry to Mr. Wonderful. He had embraced the sign of my re-entering his life as an indication that he was to commit himself to me in the midst of my cancer treatments and surgery. After my first surgery since reconnecting, Terry got down on his knee again, but this time it was in a hospital room, and he didn't have a ring. He was so eager to embrace this second chance that he wasn't willing to waste another minute on such frivolity.

Eighteen months later, we were married on December 20th in Richmond, California. He chose that day, so he would never forget our anniversary while singing "The Twelve Days of Christmas"—it would fall on the day represented with five golden rings. Our reconnecting was a miracle and is a special treasure in my heart. The gift of love—both to give and to receive—is so life-changing and life-giving.

We (and his motorcycle, a Harley wannabe) packed up and moved into a tiny rented home in a rural part of the East Bay Area. Then we embarked on new careers and mission opportunities in our community. I was the full-time director for SonShine Day Camp, which was a camp my mom and I had opened the summer before Mr. Wonderful and I reconnected. The mission of the camp was to provide care, love, and tons of character-building activities for kids in kindergarten through sixth grade. For me, it was a dream come true: I was an urban missionary on the streets where I had grown up. This outreach opportunity also introduced me to the long-term relationship I would have with parents who allowed me to borrow and love on their kids. My new husband had received army medic training in Vietnam and started working in the field of audiology.

At the time of our move, I was cancer-free, and we were working hard in our professional lives. We needed an activity that would allow us to relax and spend time together, so we repaired our motorcycle and started riding every weekend.

Eventually, Mr. Wonderful wanted something more: He had always dreamed of owning a Harley. We saved up our money for his dream bike, and after years of saving, we purchased a new, Electra Glide Classic in his favorite colors: blue and silver. This bike had a two-passenger seat, and he said he wanted this model so we could ride together more comfortably.

His excitement from seeing his dream fulfilled was contagious. The joy and anticipation from having worked so hard to make it happen was sure to bring amazing adventures. I just hoped I was still as adventurous as he was. We immediately began to plan our first, ten-day adventure within days of purchasing the Harley. We wanted to introduce our "baby" to a new country (we chose Canada) and every place along the way. The trip was amazing. I had to resist planning every detail—like lodging, meals, and stops because Mr. Wonderful said we would miss the "adventure within the adventure." What wise words!

Terry was always drawn to signs that advertised local restaurants with "the best hamburger" or any other unique attraction. He would point to the sign and say we needed to investigate, and then he'd laugh, pat my leg, and ask, "Or are we on a schedule today and have to miss it?" I finally learned that some of the best adventures come equipped with signs right in front of us that are beckoning to be seen and experienced.

After our first vacation with the new bike, we embraced the mentality and intentionality to live with a sense of spontaneity. We purposely let that sense of adventure cross into our work and ministry lives as well. On the weekends, we would carve out time to ride and pick up a map every Saturday morning. Once we decided the direction we would travel, we'd wonder what new road signs we might encounter. We could go anywhere. Our Harley brought such joy to our marriage. The riding comfort was beyond my imagination. I felt so safe riding on this bike and sitting behind Terry. It reminded us of our first ride together as freshmen in college. We became experts at packing. We only brought clothes in one color, so that if we decided to stay longer than initially planned, we wouldn't have to worry about the colors bleeding when doing laundry. This helped Terry recognize the value of detailed planning, and he learned to tolerate these habits of mine.

Our travel was always pleasant. We played our tunes on our bike and intentionally never bothered to buy an intercom system for our helmets. We communicated through touch, and it was our time only. We could not be reached by phone. Each time we were on the bike, we fell in love all over again. One of my dreams was to ride for at least eight hours, and thankfully, that was one of Terry's dreams too. I never wanted our rides to end.

We met so many people and made friends who shared life with us. Five or six homes in our neighborhood of twenty had Harley owners. We were living the dream: content in our professional lives, working hard, spending time with friends who also rode bikes, and—most importantly—we lived pain and cancer-free.

Two years after we bought the Harley, my husband received word that his company was expanding into Southern

California. He was the best candidate for a new position, and we would need to relocate at some point. The timeline was not yet determined, but the move would likely happen sometime the following year.

But wait a minute, God, my mind raged, *everything is going so great right now. He has a fulfilling job here!* I was happy serving my community and leading an ever-expanding, vacation day-camp program. I was happy serving at my church, where I interacted with the kids and was a part of their lives year-round. How could I leave the summer program and "my" kids when I had worked so hard to build a strong program? We had also just purchased a home that was nicely decorated and perfect for us ... moving simply didn't fit into our dreams. My heart cried, *Move? Really? No God, I just don't see it. You will have a lot to do to make this happen ... And seriously, you will need to show us tons of signs that you are in this.*

This was a huge decision. We needed God's clear direction, so we called a handful of people to pray on our behalf. We called another group who knew the Southern California area, so that we could look at housing and living costs, church options, etc. We prepared our hearts for God's movement, if this was the direction He was leading us in. We prayed that we would be open to a new adventure and not get crabby with one other if we didn't have the answers just yet. We prayed we wouldn't miss God in this. We asked Him specifically to help us become more aware of conversations around us that might indicate His plans for us.

As we considered the options before us, we looked at our calendar. Memorial Day weekend was coming up, and we had plans to visit friends in Southern California. Isn't it funny that our plans to visit the region had been made well before we had to face the decision to move? I love how God uses ordinary moments and makes them extraordinary—especially if you aren't expecting them. We knew at least one thing about our plans to visit Southern California: It was going to be especially important that we paid attention to the signs we'd pass on that trip.

We packed the car, prepared our hearts and minds, and left feeling excited and anxious. And God didn't disappoint. We prayed a lot more than usual on this journey compared to other vacations. The eight-hour car ride gave us plenty of time for extended prayer together. We looked at each other often and smiled, laughed, and shook our heads. We ate a lot of chocolate too.

That weekend, we visited with friends, found some good contacts for my husband, explored neighborhoods we could live in, and reported back to Terry's boss. A friend of mine was working at a church in need of a children's pastor. I wasn't looking for a job yet since we were still unsure of dates and locations. It would have been premature of me, but I knew a few other children's pastors in my circle of friends who were looking for job opportunities, so I went to the interview on their behalf to gather information. It was an impromptu meeting on a holiday weekend with their search committee, so I gathered paperwork, asked and answered questions, gave them résumés I had brought, prayed with them, and then Terry and I left and continued our vacation.

When we returned home, we reported back to our friends who had offered us guidance and who had prayed for us. We went back to our jobs and basically continued with our lives. I was facing our busiest season of twelve weeks of summer day camp. You can imagine our surprise when we received a letter from the church search committee, thanking us for meeting with them and offering me the children's pastor position. Terry and I laughed a lot. So many things were still in limbo that it didn't make sense for me to accept the job. I promptly called them and sent an email thanking them for their time and answering their offer with a resounding *no*. We received a call the next hour from the senior pastor, and he asked me to reconsider. He said they felt God was calling me to serve in their ministry. After another firm *no*, he simply asked us to pray throughout the summer and talk to them again around Labor Day.

I remember looking at my cell phone and shaking my head, wondering what part of the word *no* he didn't understand. After all, I wasn't looking for a position; I was involved in ministry in Northern California. I didn't know when (or even if) we had to move. How could this pastor know God's will for my life before I did? That wouldn't be fair, right? But I just couldn't shake the conversation, and I didn't want to ignore any signs of where God may be leading us.

Terry and I decided we would pray on this for ninety days.

We didn't know at the time that the church we had met with in Southern California was taking the same approach and committing the matter to corporate prayer. No other correspondence was exchanged between us; nothing but prayer for God to work in our hearts first if this was a glimpse of where and what He wanted for our lives.

It may sound elementary, but when we're looking for signs during a journey of any kind, we first need to be open to *seeing* those signs, and that's what prayer does for us. Prayer narrows our vision and allows us to focus on hearing His answer, but it also expands our vision and moves our hearts to think in new ways and to see things differently. His words describe this: " 'My thoughts are nothing like your thoughts,' says the LORD. 'And my ways are far beyond anything you can imagine. For just as the heavens are higher than the earth, so my ways are higher than your ways and my thoughts are higher than your thoughts' " (Isaiah 55:8–9).

I've found that when I'm in search of answers, the Scriptures come alive in new ways. What I love about God's Word is that "there is nothing new under the sun" for God (Ecclesiastes 1:9 NIV). His Word is relevant in every decision and in every circumstance. His Word provides answers for the way we should walk, the choices we should make, and the people we should surround ourselves with. It's not too old. It's not nebulous; rather, it is clear, succinct, and full of examples of people just like us traveling through this life, desiring the same things that we do—protection, security, purpose, meaning, and impact. Never in my life has there been a time when His Word has not confirmed where I should go.

I committed myself to reading the first five books of the Old Testament. So many lives are chronicled in those books, and I thought, *I want to learn how the people in Scripture followed God's Word and relied on their faith when they didn't know the result or the destination of their obedience to God.* It was faith that guided their decisions to do extraordinary things—like Noah building a boat for 120 years even when it had never rained on Earth before. And yet, Noah believed God and did what God wanted, even though it didn't make any practical sense.

God did amazing things that summer. My dream of finding people who would continue the day-camp program was realized. My staff at the church had even bigger dreams, and they took ownership of those dreams and began to lead through their passion and vision. My relationship with God was deepening as I was searching and reading His Word with new veracity. My husband and I grew closer as we sensed God had more for us. It didn't matter the location; we just wanted to be where God was at work and where our gifts, talents, and passions were needed. Our new mind-set was miraculous and brought us such contentment.

September came, and so did our annual tradition of visiting again the restaurant in Southern California where we had reconnected after fifteen years. We used the occasion to remember the gift God gave us that day. Our visit to Southern California at the end of the summer this year would be no coincidence. God had great things in store for the weekend!

I met with the senior pastor at the church that was praying for us. They had been waiting to hear whether the Lord had spoken to us about accepting their offer for me to pastor their children's ministry. I walked into my appointment with them, and eight or ten people were in the room. Their agenda was simply for us to pray together and hear what God had to say for their church and our part in it—if we had one at all. I didn't know yet what my answer would be, but I knew that if Terry and I continued to obey, pray, and read His Word, God would not let us stray off the path He had chosen for us.

Over an hour and a half later, we sensed God's call for us to move the following year. Close to that same time, Terry walked through the door and said, "I found a house. It will be available December 31st. Did you say *yes*, Linda?" Oh. My. Goodness. Tears, smiles, hugs, peace, and joy filled the room. Only God could have orchestrated this, and only God could see us through the task of uprooting our lives to serve in Southern California.

We packed up all our belongings, sold our home, said our goodbyes in Northern California, and left. We both faced transitions in our new jobs. While it was not quite the process we expected, we watched God move on our behalf. We moved into our new home on a rainy day on the very last day of the calendar year. It was hard to leave family, friends, and our first little home, but it was also exciting! Through it all, we felt peace in our hearts.

We began our new season of life and ministry by thanking God. Surrounded by the boxes containing everything we owned in this life, we reflected on how God had moved us (literally). We had been faithful to read His Word, pray, and heed wise counsel. We were so thankful for the circle of warriors around us who encouraged us in this new season.

I led an all-day seminar on the very day we moved in. We loved serving from the first day we arrived, and we continued to see God do amazing things in Huntington Beach. The people we met in those first days of ministry have been woven into the very fiber of who I am today. What marvelous blessings obedience brings when we follow the signs we encounter on our journey!

NEW PERSPECTIVES

1. When going through a challenge, look around and find those who have already walked the path you are walking.
2. Ask them for some time to share their experiences and listen to their advice.
3. If there are places you want to avoid visiting again, reevaluate any relationships or decisions you've made and want to avoid repeating in the future.
4. Choose to stop and run away from those poor decisions, and instead run toward the goals you wrote down from chapter four.

5. Take a deep breath. You are not stuck. Ask God for help. Then start again. Repeat as needed.

1

Detours and Changes

DETOURS AND CHANGES TO OUR PLANS

> You can make many plans,
> but the LORD's purpose will prevail.
> *PROVERBS 19:21*

Detour has become my favorite road sign. Although it's usually accompanied by a pile of rocks, gravel, earth, or huge equipment, this sign is almost always accompanied by big arrows pointing toward a new direction.

During our first encounter with a detour on a motorcycle, Terry and I glanced at the gas gauge, then at each other, wondering how long this detour would be. Quite frankly, we were concerned with what we could be facing. Would the weather be hotter or colder? Would the road be smooth or bumpy? Where would we end up? These were just some of the questions and considerations that rolled in our heads and showed on our faces. Detours present a whole new set of conditions, experiences, and asphalt.

I have had to learn to embrace detours as adventure. Naturally, I am a type A personality—especially when it comes to planning, so detours posed a real challenge. When we encountered these kinds of detours in the early days of our rides together, I didn't notice the road or its surroundings. I was too frustrated about the change of plan. I was too busy calculating the inconvenience, adjusting our plans, and considering how the detour would affect us (even though I couldn't really know). I would try to find someone who could provide me with the information I needed to recalculate. My poor Terry was trying to drive a Harley with a wife who was busy trying to save the world one trip at a time.

Thankfully, Terry absolutely thrived in these situations— new roads, new people to meet, new places to eat, and a new destination. He'd tell me, "Linda, just enjoy the new part of the journey. We are as prepared for this as we can be!" After I finally settled in (and that miracle took less time as we rode together more), I started to notice my surroundings. All the stories I read as a child came back to me, as I realized that I was now that missionary who would have to travel down unexpected roads.

As a side note, some of the best eateries and landscape are found on these detours. We later tried to visit these places again. We retraced the detour to locate them, but our surroundings were no longer familiar. The road was newly paved, and signs no longer marked the detour. It was one of these such instances when we realized the true gift of the detour.

Not all detours are necessarily worth revisiting. Such was the case for me on a mid-September morning seventeen years into my marriage with Terry. I kissed him goodbye at six o'clock in the morning that day before he got on his motorcycle to travel with his friend to Reno, Nevada. They would attend Street Vibrations, a weekend event that brings together all kinds of people riding all kinds of bikes. The trek to get there would require about ten hours of riding through the not-so-scenic parts of California.

This was a planned, ten-day vacation and adventure we would take with another couple. The event ran from Thursday through Sunday, and we always made new friends among the thousands of bikers and riders who swelled the city. Terry and I had attended this annual event when we lived in the San Francisco area even before we owned a Harley, and we wanted to share this event with our Southern California friends.

The plan was set: We would leave on Thursday morning at six in order to beat Los Angeles traffic. We'd stop for breakfast two hours later and get off the bike every hundred miles to stretch and refuel. We would arrive in Reno around four in the afternoon, wash the bikes, then ourselves, and finally settle in. The fun part would come after all of that when we would check in at Street Vibrations for passes, parking permits, and the weekend's agenda. Then we would go downtown, park the bike, meet people, and enjoy four days of fun!

After the Street Vibrations event had ended on Sunday, we would say goodbye to our friends and head to the Bay Area to visit family (and do some much-needed laundry). We would leave the Bay Area on Monday morning without an itinerary and arrive home in Southern California the following Saturday. This would leave us enough time to attend church on Sunday morning and then spend the afternoon preparing for work on Monday. It was a perfect plan.

However, the weekend prior to our departure, I spoke at the women's retreat at our church. With each day of the retreat, I began to feel weaker. It was warm, but we were busy having fun—reuniting with friends and making new ones. God was moving out of our conversations and into our hearts. I loved this weekend of not only teaching but also receiving profound wisdom from other women who spoke and sang and lived the seasons of life. The days were long, and the evenings were short. You'd think we were at a slumber party or something! I made it through and returned home late Sunday afternoon. I went straight to bed after kissing Terry hello and goodnight.

I made a call to my doctor on Monday morning. She examined me and then sent me straight to the hospital for refueling. I had become dehydrated and needed fluids. The hospital kept me into the early evening, and then I was instructed to go home and rest—especially since I would be leaving on Thursday morning for a long motorcycle ride.

Fast forward to Wednesday night at six when I received a call from my doctor. She wanted me to consider flying to Reno on Thursday with Stacey, the wife of the couple with whom we'd be spending the weekend and who was already planning on flying, instead of riding. I understood my doctor's thinking; she wanted me to take an extra day of rest since I would be riding all the other days. I knew she was looking out for my physical well-being, but I *loved* being on a bike for hours at a time. Those hours gave me time to unplug and reconnect with Terry, both of which fed my heart and soul. But on the extremely practical level, her suggestion made sense. I called the airline Stacey was flying with and was able to book a seat next to her. My bags were packed and put onto the motorcycle, so that when we arrived that afternoon to meet our husbands, I would be ready for our ten days of adventure. The kid in me didn't want to miss out on traveling by bike, but the grown-up in me knew this was the smarter choice.

Our alarm went off on Thursday morning at five. We awoke in each other's arms feeling so very thankful for the life we were living. We prayed as we normally did and added a request that the Lord would put a hedge of protection around the guys and the wives since we were traveling separately this day. We showered, brewed a pot of coffee, and finished packing our things on, in, and around the bike. Our friend pulled into the driveway on his bike with a roar. Before my eyes were two grown men who were as excited as two little boys waiting for an ice cream truck. They could not wipe those huge smiles off their faces, and that just delighted my heart.

Off they went, pipes waking the neighbors as they pulled

onto the street for their adventure. Two hours later, they called to let me know they were sitting down for breakfast. They had covered more distance than I thought they would in those first two hours. Their laughter was so contagious over the phone that I couldn't help but smile.

My day wouldn't be filled with much laughter or adventure, as I still had a couple of hours of work, yet I was filled with hope because I would join Stacey at the airport later that afternoon and have a brief layover at a smaller airport before arriving in Reno around five that evening. It was a warm day with the promise of an awesome weekend. We were ready!

Stacey and I were so excited to board the plane. No sooner had the plane leveled off at our cruising altitude than the flight was landing. The four of us had not made prior arrangements to connect during our layover, so we knew our chances of reaching them were slim. They were on their bikes and wearing helmets, so there was really no way for them to even hear their phones ring. But that didn't stop us from trying.

I dialed Terry's number, and he answered! They had stopped at a store on the border of California and Nevada just twelve miles from our hotel in Reno. I will always remember how our conversation began:

"Hey there, honey," I said. "I am so glad I got you on the phone. We just wanted to check in on you guys and hear about your ride."

"I'm so glad you called, love," Terry returned. "We are doing great and are almost home."

"Home?" I asked. "Are you back in Orange County? Did you have any problems?" I suddenly worried about what could have happened.

"Oh no!" he replied quickly, "I meant we are just a few miles away from the hotel."

"Whew! I'm so glad about that! We have another thirty minutes before we board. I missed being on this ride with you, and I can't wait to see you."

"Yes," Terry said, "I am feeling the same way. I can't believe I have driven this last five hundred plus miles without you. We've always shared the journey and the miles."

"Yup, we have. And I have enjoyed it. You have shown me places I would have never seen otherwise," I told him as memories flooded my mind.

"The perspective you continually bring to my life is unmatched," Terry said. "I was thinking today while driving how miraculous it was for us to even meet over the phone your first week at Biola—sight unseen! Getting engaged. Getting my military orders. Getting un-engaged. Seeing you from across the room at a restaurant fifteen years later. We have been blessed to have had the best ride ever just as God ordained for us: being married and sharing our lives and ministry for the last seventeen years." Then he said, "Never forget, you have always had my heart!"

"You are God's personal gift to me," I responded. "I will never forget! I have to make my way to the gate now. I'll see you in less than an hour."

"Babe, there will be a surprise waiting for you when you arrive," Terry said.

"Wow! That sounds pretty awesome!" I exclaimed. "I look forward to seeing you and being in your arms."

"Remember babe, I love you!" he said. "Only you!"

"I can't wait to see you," I assured him.

"We will see one another face-to-face," Terry said, "and I look forward to that as I ride these last few miles."

And with that, we ended our conversation.

Stacey and I boarded the plane and, as the plane started to leave the runway at 4:10 p.m., a small gasp escaped my lips. For a moment, I wondered what our conversation could have meant but the rest of the flight was uneventful. As Stacey went to collect her luggage and since mine was on Terry's bike, I looked out the windows for the guys. I wondered what surprise Terry had arranged for our arrival. Our imaginations ran wild thinking that perhaps they had arranged for the hotel shuttle, which was a limo, to pick us up. We have great imaginations.

There was no limo or hotel shuttle, and I didn't hear loud pipes either. I felt like a woman at the door of her favorite store—minutes before it opens, and tapping her fingers on the glass and saying, "Open, open, open." We waited, but nobody came for us. Stacey called her husband, Frank, but it went to his voicemail. I called Terry and got his voicemail too.

We hailed a taxi to bring us to our hotel. When we arrived at the Atlantis Hotel and Casino, we approached the concierge desk, expecting our husbands to have already checked in. But the concierge said no one had checked in. That was certainly odd. They were "almost home," as Terry said just ninety minutes ago when they were just a few miles from the hotel. We were sure there must have been a mistake and asked the concierge to check again. She ran both of our names, and after watching her tap on the keyboard for a few minutes, her answer was the same: "No one has checked in."

We tried calling them again but only got their voicemail. We looked at each other, unsure of what to do next. It was then that we looked up and saw two older couples approaching us. Their faces looked so sad and so very serious, and we knew something had happened. It seemed they had something to say to us, but what? Stacey and I glanced at each other, but neither of us recognized them. Emotions started to flood our minds. They still hadn't said anything to us, but then one of the ladies took my hand, and her husband put his hand on my shoulder. Whatever it was, it had to do with me.

They asked us if we had checked into our room yet, and we said we had not. One couple left and approached the desk to have a conversation with the hotel clerk we had spoken to minutes before. The other couple had not spoken a word to us yet and just stood there sadly with us. When the first couple returned, they handed us our keys and said they had checked us in upstairs. But we didn't move. We were just standing there and listening to strangers without any idea as to why they were there, or why they were taking such an interest in helping us.

We politely asked if we knew them, or if perhaps they were

friends of someone we knew. They had received a call from Pastor Hous, and he was coming to be with us. With a growing sense of alarm, both Stacey and I asked at the same time, "Why? What happened?"

They said there had been an accident, and they would like to speak with us further. They suggested we go to our room to continue the conversation. As we took the elevator up to the seventeenth floor, I don't recall any words were spoken. We silently exited the elevator, found the room, and entered. Stacey and I sat next to each other on a bed, and one of the couples sat on the other bed across from me and again took my hand. I remember looking straight ahead at the man who was speaking, and he repeated that he had received a call from Pastor Hous. Only this time, he continued the story and told us Pastor Hous had received a call from Stacey's husband, Frank. There had been an accident on Highway 80, just outside Reno.

We asked if the guys were okay and what hospital they were at. After a long silence that seemed to go on forever, he lifted his eyes and looked directly at me. He said my husband had passed on the highway. Not fully comprehending what he meant by the word "passed," I asked him, "What exactly do you mean?"

He quietly told me that my husband had passed away on Highway 80. He said Frank was still with Terry on the side of the highway. I remember Stacey immediately stood and tried to call Frank. I looked up at her, hoping what this older gentleman was telling me was not true. I wanted desperately to believe this was all just a dream, as my perfect world began to turn dark.

I fought the tears rolling down my cheeks because this couldn't be true! This had to be a mistake. Even as I write about this moment years later, my tears run down my face uncontrollably and drip onto my keyboard.

I remember becoming numb, and the room started to spin. Every other sound in the room faded into silence. Stacey looked at me with tears in her eyes. She still had not been able to reach Frank on the phone. I told Stacey and these couples this was clearly a mistake; we had spoken to them just two hours ago. I started to pace around the room—after all, I couldn't just sit there. I picked up my phone and called Terry. It went to his voicemail, and I heard his voice. These people must have received incorrect information. This could not be true. My husband, Mr. Wonderful, was bigger than life; this just *could not* be true.

There was a knock at the door. One of the wives let the chaplain of the Reno police force inside. He was a man with kind eyes, and he brought a sense of peace with him as he walked through the door. I asked him why he was here with us. He said he was here to speak to the wife of Terry Vannoy. I had always been happy to be referred to as "the wife of Terry Vannoy" until that moment. Those words from the chaplain brought a somber, sinking feeling. The news I had already heard was about to be confirmed as reality.

The chaplain sat across from me and took both of my hands into his. He looked deeply into my eyes and told me gently and quietly that my husband had passed away on the highway, and that his body was being transferred to a morgue as we spoke. Terry had been hit by a camper and run over by an eighteen-wheeler truck.

I didn't hear another word even though his lips kept moving. Images and questions flashed through my heart and mind. *Was it painful? Did he feel any of those hits? What went through his mind when he was lying on the highway? Did his friend see all of this? Was Frank hit too? Did Frank see him die? Did my husband say anything to him? Did my husband know that he wasn't alone? Why did God take me off this bike twenty-four hours before? Did Terry suffer?*

A touch on my hand brought me back to my awareness of the room. The chaplain had something he wanted me to hear. He asked if Frank had returned yet, and Stacey said, "No." He looked at both of us and said Frank never left Terry's side—from the moment of impact until authorities arrived to pick up his body. The chaplain told Stacey that he expected Frank to arrive soon.

As we sat together, the chaplain asked if we could pray together. He told us he was here so that we would not be alone as we heard the news and to assist us with anything we would need. He came to help us remember God. I could not breathe. I could barely think as tears rolled down my cheeks.

I had trouble sorting through my emotions and the information. I couldn't seem to vocalize a question or even a thought. I felt mute or broken in some way as nothing came out. All I could do was sit there with my hands folded in my lap, not believing these people and their words—these awful, untrue words.

Then Frank walked in. He was still wearing his leathers and holding his helmet. He looked beat. His eyes were swollen, and he entered slowly, looking first at Stacey, and then kneeling before me, mumbling over and over, "I am sorry, Linda. He was never alone; I stayed with him. I am sorry, Linda. He was never alone; I stayed with him."

I looked at him and lifted his head in my hands. I asked, "Is it really true? Is he really gone? What happened?"

I hardly recall his answers, even to this day, but I do remember his eyes. They confirmed my worst fears. I'm sure the conversation around me continued, but all I can recall after that moment is that I tried to be brave and sat completely still. I hoped against hope that if I didn't acknowledge all these conversations, then perhaps they would not be true.

So I sat, and I sat until Stacey put her hand on mine and told me the chaplain was going to take us to the morgue to collect Terry's things. We didn't have sufficient transportation for all of us, so the chaplain would drive us. I realized I had no clothes since they were packed on the motorcycle. The chaplain made a call and said we would stop by the salvage yard, where Terry's motorcycle was, to collect my things. He committed himself to us for the evening and ensured everything we needed was taken care of.

The couples were pastors, and now that we were in good

hands with the chaplain, they said they would be leaving. After they left, the chaplain sat at the desk by the hotel window and started to make calls.

I walked like a zombie to my bathroom and looked in the mirror. *This cannot be true. This has to be a dream—and a bad one at that,* I said to myself. I bent over the sink and sobbed while I tried to splash water on my face. My mind knew it was true because the people I loved had just told me, but my heart held out hope that they were wrong. If only it would be that this mistake were cleared up when we got to the morgue and discovered the accident victim wasn't Terry. We would shake off these awful moments and get back to life as we had planned it.

When everything you thought you knew is shattered, thoughts race through your mind. I kept taking deep breaths because I felt weak, dizzy, and unable to let this kind of information seep into my brain. I didn't want my reality to change; I wanted everything the way it was before. *Why, God? Why?* my mind screamed over and over.

There was a knock on the bathroom door. It was Stacey, and she said it was time to go. I could see she had been crying and was concerned for me. I let her take my arm and lead me to where the chaplain stood, and then together we left the hotel. I remember seeing all the Harleys in the parking lot of the Atlantis Hotel. The bikes looked clean and shiny; men and women wearing leathers were talking loudly, laughing, and slapping each other on the back.

"Terry and I should be there with you and Frank," I told

Stacey as we got into the chaplain's car. I sat still and quiet as I stared out the window of the backseat at all the people. I just knew we should be there, and all of this was a misunderstanding. I remember praying to God to make all this disappear and help us find Terry. God was the only truth I have ever known, and I needed Him to show up for me—right now!

We arrived at a locked building, and the chaplain called someone. A man with a file and a manila envelope came to the door. He invited everyone into a room on our left. We sat around a metal table, and I suddenly felt cold. I heard low conversation between Frank and the coroner. Then the coroner opened his file and told me my husband was hit, and much of the report of his injuries had been taken down and confirmed by Frank at the scene. I just had to identify the body, review the report, and collect the things from inside the envelope that sat on the table before me.

Frank cleared his throat and asked if his identification of Terry on the scene would be enough for the official record. Frank told the coroner he didn't feel it was necessary for me to see the state of Terry's body after the accident. Frank then turned to me and asked if I would be comfortable letting him identify Terry's body.

I wanted to be listed on the official record as the person who identified Terry's body, and I thought I could do it. After all, Terry would do the same for me. But something about Frank's manner and expression led me to trust him with the task. Later, I learned from Frank that Terry's body having been dragged by the camper and run over by the eighteen-wheeler was an image that would have haunted me. I instantly felt saddened that Frank would always have that image in his head and heart. I saw then as I still see today—almost twelve years later—God's profound protection for me. I still pray often for my friend and ask God to erase that image for Frank.

I know many more words were spoken, but I didn't hear a thing. I sat quietly at the table, sliding my husband's wedding ring on and off of my finger and remembering our wedding day. Then I opened his wallet and felt assaulted by its familiar smell, and I held his keys. The tears would not stop falling.

I had to sign papers, and I remember laughing at some of the questions they asked me. I'm sure it was nervous laughter, but the routine questions struck me as ridiculous.

"Do you have a favorite funeral home here in Reno?"

I thought, *Seriously? I have traveled to many towns and cities, and never have I checked out the local funeral homes.* Out loud I said, "What would you suggest?"

The coroner handed me a list.

"How do you imagine having Terry transported to your home?"

Again, I thought, *Well, I had just planned for us to ride up to Reno and then home on the Harley. This has been quite a change of my plans.* Instead, I asked, "What are my options?"

The coroner said, "Well, you can transport him, but the charge to transport bodies is calculated by the pound."

More nervous laughter. He was about 185 pounds.

I then asked, "What if I cremated him? Would that cost less money?"

"Yes," the coroner said, "but only the US Postal Service can transport him, as remains are considered hazardous material."

Still more nervous laughter from me.

"If you want cremation," the coroner continued, "then this would be the funeral home I suggest."

"Good," I said and then asked, "What do I do now?"

"I will contact the funeral home tonight," he explained. "We need to move his body within the next twenty-four hours according to state law. The state will contact you to confirm financial and shipping arrangements." Then he asked, "Would you care to make other arrangements, like transporting the body over the state line yourself?"

I turned to Frank and said, "Hey, Frank, do you still have bungee cords on your bike? Do you think maybe we could put Terry's body on the back of your bike, wrap him in a bungee cord, and watch him move about—arms and legs moving freely—just like *Weekend at Bernie's,* and get him to the California state line at Lake Tahoe?" It was sick of me to say, I know, but it brought a shred of levity to the room. It was just too traumatic a time to be making these decisions. Information needed to be gathered, and I was so thankful I had my friends there to navigate these waters with me—even my sad attempts at humor.

The coroner excused himself for about thirty minutes but asked us to wait while the arrangements were put into motion.

Left in the room with my friends and their somber faces, the reality of my beloved's death began to sink in. I felt cold again and realized no one in my family had been notified. I hadn't allowed myself to believe he was truly gone, so I had seen no reason to call anyone.

I needed to call Terry's family and grieve together. What would I say? What could I possibly say to a mother who has just lost her son? How many phone calls would I have to make? How many times would I have to relive the tragic sequence of events? I was all alone. We had no children. We had godchildren who attended different churches. We were part of a large community of friends in Southern California, so I knew many of our friends would hear the news without me having to contact them directly. I was grateful to learn our church already knew about Terry's passing, since Frank had called Pastor Hous. They notified Terry's mom in-person at the same time I was told by the pastors in Reno.

No longer a wife. No longer married; this was the moment of "until death do us part." I was now a widow who had arrangements to make. I didn't know how to do this. I slowly stood up from my chair, exited the room, and stood in the lobby of the coroner's building. I pulled my phone out of my purse and called my mom, Terry's mom, and Wanda and Tralee, two of my godchildren's moms. I cried through each one of the calls and felt exhausted by the time I finished around eight o'clock that night. Each phone call I made launched another series of phone calls, and a growing number of people prayed for me.

The chaplain, Frank, and Stacey came out with the coroner and met me in the lobby shortly after I had finished my calls. I didn't know quite what to say except to express my profound thanks in caring for my husband that night. It took all the energy I had to quietly thank the chaplain for helping me process the next steps.

We got into the chaplain's car to head to the salvage yard for my clothes, money, and toiletries we had packed on Terry's motorcycle just fifteen hours before. I wasn't sure what condition the bike would even be in. I had never felt so out of control of my surroundings as I did that evening. I felt emotionally pelted from every angle and overwhelming exhaustion and numbness. Yet my heart felt like it was breaking apart. I could visualize pieces of it falling off a deep cliff. I felt like I would throw myself down that same deep cliff at any minute. My head spun, and a headache started to form. I tried not to cry. My friends had seen enough—too much, in fact. I felt I should try to help them through all of this. At times throughout the drive, I lost my breath.

We pulled into what looked like a junkyard and tons of lights were on. We silently followed the chaplain until he entered the junkyard's office, and we waited outside while he handled the details. Upon his return, we were ushered into a brightly lit room filled with cars, bikes, machinery, and tools. I smelled oil and grease. We were introduced to the man who appeared to be in charge. His kind eyes saw me and my breaking heart. Quietly, he led me to that beautiful blue and silver

Electra Glide. My hands gingerly touched the seat where my husband had been sitting just five hours ago. Marks from the impact of trucks and the sliding on asphalt covered the bike. The chrome and handlebars were mangled and twisted.

Tears began to flow silently at first, and then I heard air escape my mouth. I just couldn't be that brave wife I knew Terry would want me to be. I worked hard to control my imagination and struggled to stop the images of my beloved's body and bike twisted and torn. I hadn't seen any photographs from the scene; I was left with my imagination. I grasped the handlebars, closed my eyes, and sensed his presence—his last breath, his last hope to "cheat death once again," which was a favorite saying of his. Time stopped. Other people were in the room, but I was unaware of any movement.

The gentleman silently offered me my bag of clothing and my other things. I lifted my eyes to find a way to thank him. I didn't want to leave. I wanted to sleep here, holding this bike. Holding Terry. The man in the garage handed me another bag that contained Terry's things. I immediately raised Terry's jacket to my nose to smell him. Again, my heart strained to hope that he was in a hospital somewhere. Between the smell of him and the knowledge of his death, I felt confused. Honestly, I couldn't understand how both things could co-exist. Yet deep down, I knew he was gone. Deep down, I knew I would never be the same again. Deep down, I didn't care about anything. Deep down, I knew a huge part of me had died with Terry. We had been so close that I couldn't discern where he started and I ended. Our lives were so intertwined that I didn't know how I was going to even survive without him—in that moment I wasn't sure I really wanted to.

We said our goodbyes. My last glance at our bike brought an onslaught of memories from our rides together. They raced through my mind with such speed that I could barely see them or even speak of their significance, but each one mattered: From the day we purchased the bike and his huge smile as he drove home, to our drive onto a ferry boat and into Canada, our drive through the Redwoods on those curvy roads, our changing into leathers on the cold, damp Oregon Coast, and his departure with Frank that morning.

That was just this morning. The thought struck me again. *How will I get through tonight? How will I sleep knowing he will never lie next to me in bed again? How can I do this? I don't know how. I just don't know how.*

When we got back into the car to return to the hotel, my phone, which I left in the car while we were in the garage, was blowing up with text messages, missed calls, and voicemails. I methodically listened to each message and read each text, feeling helpless. How would I even get back to all these people? Stacey sat next to me and faced the same challenge. Many of the people from our home church were encouraging, supporting, and helping her walk through this evening, and many were contacting her to find out how I was doing.

We arrived at the hotel and said goodbye to the chaplain who had been an awesome godsend. We decided we needed to finally eat something. I don't remember having much of an appetite, and soon we were back in our rooms. We said our goodnights and closed the door between us. So much had happened in the last few hours that my brain was having trouble recalling and storing all the information. I busied myself getting ready for bed. I checked my phone again for messages before attempting to sleep and returned only one message to my former pastor and friend, David Fasold of Bay Hills Community Church, who wanted to know how I was really doing and whether he should fly out to me. I said *yes*.

As I turned off the lights and crawled into bed, tears would not stop coming. My face was wet; my neck and pillow were soaked. I sat up in bed and tried to figure out what to do next. Then my phone rang. My friend Tralee and another friend's husband, George, had driven up to see me. It was midnight. The Atlantis hotel was booked solid for the Street Vibrations' annual event, but because Terry had worked in the Reno area for six to eight weeks every year and only stayed at the Atlantis, everyone from the staff—the front desk attendants, servers, dealers, and pit bosses knew and loved him. When the hotel managers heard what had happened, they blocked out rooms for my family and friends to stay in at no cost.

Tralee and George had dropped everything in their lives at a moment's notice to travel to be with me. What amazing friends! But I didn't feel ready to see them just yet. It was too soon. I felt like raw meat; I couldn't tell if I hurt more than I was angry. I didn't understand any of this. Through gasps and tears, I stalled our meeting. Part of me wanted to be held and told everything would be alright. But I also wanted to be strong. I wanted to experience this with honor and dignity, but all I could do was cry, sniffle, blow my nose, and repeat. Between ragged breaths I asked them to come to my room at five thirty in the morning, which would give me five hours to get it together.

Then I noticed from across the room that the door adjoining my room to Frank and Stacey's was open again. I closed the door so Stacey and Frank could sleep; I didn't want them to worry about me. Their hearts were broken; I could see that. I needed to not be selfish. After I closed the door, I found myself grabbing the blanket and pillow from my bed. I walked into the bathroom, wrapped myself in the blanket, and crawled into the tub. I bent over with the pillow between my knees and wailed, cried, and cried some more. I didn't want anyone to hear my private hell. I knew I couldn't go on. I didn't want to go on. I was scared. I was alone. No one could walk this for me. There were no substitutions. It was on me to make my husband's life a legacy. I needed to be brave and strong, and remember to reflect Jesus well.

These thoughts stopped me, helped me breathe, and brought peace. I still hurt, and I still cried, but I remembered that I was not alone. I remembered God is the God of all comfort. His Spirit was with me, and I could go on. I climbed out of the tub. Frank or Stacey had reopened the door between our rooms, and I closed it again. I laid in bed and fell asleep. I woke up after four hours of sleep and wanted to have a conversation with God before I was to meet with Tralee.

Although I had slept in complete peace, I knew it was important for me to meet with Him as I had done every day since I was eight years old. Each morning, I had a date with God around five thirty when I would read His Word and pray. I also had quiet time to listen to Him speak to me through His Word and through my various thoughts. Today would be no different, except I would share my hurt, angry, confused, and broken heart and wait for Him to talk to me.

I needed wisdom. I needed help. He knew where I was, and He knew me. We had gone through stuff together before. I desperately needed Him. However, I knew the rules would now be different, or at least I thought so. My heart had changed. I didn't know how to even walk in this new day. I had two Bible passages in my mind as I walked toward the window, but the door connecting our suites was open again. I closed it. This conversation needed to be private.

As I stood at my window and looked out at the mountains surrounding Reno, Nevada, on the seventeenth floor, these verses came to mind: "I look up to the mountains—does my help come from there? My help comes from the LORD, who made heaven and earth!" (Psalm 121:1–2). And "The faithful love of the LORD never ends! His mercies never cease. Great is his faithfulness; his mercies begin afresh each morning" (Lamentations 3:22–23).

I took a deep breath after reciting these words out loud

and basically stood with my hands on my hips with an attitude. My posture showed that my heart was so broken it felt like it was turning cold inside of me. I then started to cry out audibly to the Lord, "My heart hurts, Lord. I can't even feel my heart anymore. I didn't see this coming; this is too much for me to bear. Why did you take me off the bike? Maybe I could have helped. I don't think I can do this. Terry was much stronger than me."

Louder, I said, "I need your help. That's why I am here this morning. I remember memorizing your Word, and these verses promise you can help me. I am looking at the mountains; you created the heavens and the earth. You can bring Terry back to life, and you are present. You are faithful and new every morning. I am here telling you—yes, you, almighty God—I can't do this. I can't do anything the way I have always done things, and that includes our relationship.

"I have no husband who will hold me through the night. I have no husband who will wake with me, kiss me, and tell me that he loves me or start our day in prayer. You took him. You took him. And I wasn't even there! So now, God, it's all going to fall on you. You will have to hold me. You will have to pray for me. You will have to tell me that you love me more than anything. You are going to have to come after me. Starting tomorrow morning, I will wait for you at this same time at this window. I will not bring my Bible. I am asking you to remind me of passages that I have memorized, and that you give me the Scripture I'll need for each of my days ahead. I want your private attention."

And with those final words, I walked away from the window, took a shower, and readied myself to meet Tralee and all that was ahead of me. I had never spoken to the Lord this way. Oh, I had whined and cried out desperately before, but I had never demanded my way so strongly. I knew that my God was big enough to take my hurts, brokenness, stubbornness, and questions and not just zap me into oblivion. He lets me speak out, cry out, and be silent. I would wait for Him tomorrow morning (hopefully not too angrily).

At 5:30 that morning, Tralee came in followed by George, Frank, Stacey, my brother and sister-in-law, my former pastor David, and thirty other friends, teens, and kids who wanted to hold me, love me, cry with me, laugh with me, eat with me, and share stories they had of Mr. Wonderful. People drove in from the San Francisco Bay Area, and there were countless phone calls, texts, messages, pictures, emails, and conversations from all over the world—and this was before I even had a Facebook account. The Atlantis provided us with a morning brunch and an area for us to be for the next twenty-four hours. It was wonderful to not have to walk this alone.

At eleven thirty that morning, I had an appointment with the funeral home that would cremate Terry, so we needed to make arrangements. The family and friends who helped make these decisions were such a gift. I mean, I just wanted Terry alive again. How much did I have to arrange to have that happen? I was so thankful that Terry was a veteran, and Frank could set up the burial arrangements for me in Southern

California. I had to select and purchase an urn. I had to pay for his care in the funeral home when the coroner delivered Terry to them. I decided to do two funeral services: One at my current church in Southern California, and the other at my former church in Northern California. Fortunately, the decisions about those services did not have to be made that morning.

So many people came to Reno that day, so I had to ask if we could have some sort of viewing for Mr. Wonderful. The gentleman at the funeral home made some calls and eventually said yes. He said Terry would need a shirt, at least, and did I have one? My heart thought, *Now, I will get to see my beloved.* I went to his bag in the closet, pulled out one of his favorites, and gave it to the funeral home consultant. He folded it neatly and set it on his binders, took my check, and left.

The thought hit me again, *He is gone, isn't he? Will this be the last time I will see his face?* My friends saw my expression and seemed to read my thoughts. They slowly and quietly left the room. Only Tralee and Wanda stayed with me. We sat on the beds in silence for a while. They suggested we eat and let everyone know of the three o'clock service. News traveled among the Atlantis staff as well, and they were stopping in our area near the buffet the Atlantis had set up for us. Their hugs, tears, silent presence, and knowing looks helped. I went back upstairs to shower and get ready.

I felt like I was in a trance. This tropical-paradise-themed hotel lacked color for me. It looked so black and white. But I was not alone—God, my family, and my friends were all around me. I would do this in His strength alone because mine was gone! We arrived at the funeral home, and they had a lovely chapel. Light streamed through the many windows. Friends and family took their seats in the pews. It seemed like each friend and each family had their own row with their own thoughts.

I was (and still am) so grateful my former pastor was there. He spoke for a few moments while music played softly in the background then invited everyone to approach Terry's casket and spend as much time as they wanted or needed with him. I stood in the back. I couldn't sit down. I didn't want people to shake my hand as they paid their respects. It was hard enough to watch people look so lovingly into his face, hold his hand, touch his head, and cry. These were my family, friends, god-children, kids, and teens—all of them impacted by his life. I was nervous. I tried to wear an outfit that would make him proud, but I had packed for a vacation, not a funeral.

What would I say to my beloved? What words would wake him up? Is this really goodbye? Why won't these tears stop? Pastor David came along beside me to let me know that the chapel was empty, and it was now my turn to see Terry. *Where did everyone go?* I wondered. I had just been looking at them, but thirty minutes had passed while I was caught up in personal reflections. The workers at the funeral home looked at me with such sadness in their eyes, and they didn't even know him.

I walked slowly down the aisle between the pews. I saw him lying in the casket. I could see his face. His shirt. His head didn't turn to me as I called out his name. I could barely see anything through my tears. *Does he even know that I am here with him?* I wondered. Sobs erupted, and I couldn't breathe. I grabbed a nearby chair and set it beside him and the borrowed casket. Before I sat down, I called to my beloved one final time and placed my hand on his cheek. His skin was so cold. I put my hand on his chest. He was cold there too. I couldn't sit down; I longed to lie next to him. I reached for his hand, but it didn't reach out to meet me as it always used to do. Grief overcame my thoughts, my words, and my heart.

Oh God, he is truly gone from me. Can't you just give me another five minutes? God was silent.

Mr. Wonderful was silent. I collapsed into the chair holding my arms with my head tucked into my chest. I could barely breathe as I sobbed ugly tears. Then I had a thought: *I know how I can wake him. I will tell Terry that I have his gold disco chain from the '80s that he hated.* We had just found it a week earlier. He said he wouldn't be caught dead wearing it. *I will threaten him that it's in my purse, and I'm going to put it on him.*

I said those words aloud, opened up my purse and pretended to look for it. When I looked up, he wasn't sitting up and grinning like he used to, with a smile so huge that it made his beautiful blue eyes nearly disappear. In that moment I knew he was gone—really gone. He would never return to this world or to me. It was such a silly but intimate moment between him and me.

I looked lovingly at him, held his hand, and through

broken sobs spoke to him, "You promised that I would never die alone. You promised that you would never leave me. Is this the surprise you told me I would be prepared for? I am sorry, honey, but I don't like this surprise. I am sorry that I don't think I am strong enough to be without you, without your love for me—living in me—without your daily prayers for me. Without you."

Silence. Quiet tears. I stood up and laid my head on his chest. His big heart was silent. My tears were wetting his shirt. I kissed him goodbye until we would meet again in eternity. I looked at him—willing him to waken, but this time I knew he was gone and would not awaken here. He was already awake in his new home, hopefully with a new Harley, and checking out the golden roads, and taking people on rides to new adventures.

When I walked out of those doors and into the warmth of Nevada's afternoon sun, I knew I too would be going on new adventures. I would never have chosen this road, but I knew that despite my brokenness, I would one day be whole again. Although I was lonely for my Mr. Wonderful, I was not alone. I was hurt, but I would heal. Definitely not that day, and probably not the next one either, but the sting would eventually go away. I wasn't sure when that day would come, but I knew that it would!

All thirty-five of us met back at our little corner of the buffet area at the Atlantis hotel for more hugs, tears, and silent companionship. Perhaps we were all trying to wrap our heads around the loss of the man who had squeezed himself into our hearts. Some people had to board planes, gas up their cars, and return to their everyday lives. A part of me wanted to hold this moment in my heart and not let anyone disappear, but a part of me knew it was time for some to leave. I envied their returning to life as usual when I knew that my life would be forever changed. A part of me was screaming inside for everything to go back to the way it was yesterday morning; another part of me sighed heavily, knowing that my tomorrow would probably hurt as much as this morning had.

I ate dinner with my brother, Earl, and my sister-in-law, Dee. I was eating solely out of my body's need for nutrition, as I still had no appetite. I wanted their company, but I couldn't find words that did not revolve around my sudden loss, so we said little during the meal. After they left, Pastor David came to sit with us before he left for his flight. We talked about a formal service for Terry the following weekend and the details of the service. He took notes and assured me he would arrange it. We confirmed the date of my return to the Bay Area before Terry's celebration service and arranged when we would meet with Terry's family. I remember thinking to myself that my time with them would be a good opportunity to gather input from his mom and family on how I would present Terry's life at the service. I hoped this process would allow my shattered heart to heal.

I suddenly felt tired after that discussion. Those who were with me encouraged me to return to my room and rest. Some of my friends would stay the night. Wanda got "Linda duty" or drew the "short straw" as I call it, although she said she wanted to stay close and watch over me. Both of the rooms adjoining mine were used by people who were staying. Wanda and I shared lots of conversation, laughter, and girlfriend time that went into the late hours of the evening.

I spent many more moments in the tub—wrapped in a blanket and with my pillow. Early in the morning, I saw that blasted door that connected our rooms was open again, and most of my friends were sleeping next door. Only Wanda was in my room. I must have kept her awake throughout most of the night because each time I came out of the bathroom wrapped in my blanket, she was looking at me. No words, just looking at me with sadness and concern. I crawled into bed hoping I would be able to sleep—sleep away this awful dream that had become a living nightmare.

NEW PERSPECTIVES

1. Look for detours in your life that offer greater adventure. Grab hold of them and enjoy those unplanned moments.

2. Have you experienced any detours that changed the very fabric of who you are? Take a moment to journal any questions you have for God about those detours.

3. Do you have a need to plan things out? If so, does this tendency prevent you from embracing detours and new and experiences, or does it allow you to see the beauty around you even while adjusting your plans?

8

Riding Together Is Better Than Riding Alone

THE IMPORTANCE OF SUPPORT FROM OTHERS

If you have men who will only come
if they know there is a good road,
I don't want them. I want men who
will come if there is no road at all.

DAVID LIVINGSTONE

*A*t four thirty in the morning on my second day as a widow, I woke and sat straight up in bed. Wanda, for the first time all night, looked like she was asleep. I went to the window where I had spoken to God so sternly. I wondered if He would come to me. I needed to be held this morning. I needed Him to tell me that He loved me. I needed to be seen—not just as a broken widow, but to really be seen like I had value and mattered.

I had spoken to Him with such firmness yesterday. Maybe I had scared Him off. Maybe I wasn't respectful enough. Maybe He would just teach me a lesson and stay away for a bit. But suddenly the fountains and the lighting changed below me. Birds were flying everywhere as if they were dancing, and I suddenly felt a presence. I looked over to see if Wanda was standing near me, but she was still asleep in bed. I looked back down at the fountain and the dancing birds, and I heard a voice speak words I had learned long ago:

> Look at the birds. They don't plant or harvest or store food in barns, for your heavenly Father feeds them. And aren't you far more valuable to him than they are? ... So don't worry about tomorrow, for tomorrow will bring its own worries. Today's trouble is enough for today. (Matthew 6:26, 34)

I turned around instantly to see who it was. I heard an audible voice—not something in my head or heart. Tears streamed down my face as the voice continued: He had come to me. He spoke love to me. He said that I had value. He said that He would take care of me. He told me not to worry about the future; all that mattered for this moment was that He would help me through today. I could feel the embrace of His presence. I was seen. I mattered. The God who created the heavens and earth, the one who I had called out to so desperately the previous morning was there to meet me. He called to me. I think that's why I awoke sitting straight up in bed. He had met my terms with His Word. And now I could face the day with the promises He gave to me.

I leaned up beside the window, waiting for my instructions. What did I need to do today? And as suddenly as He spoke, I knew what to do—I knew! I spent a few moments silently speaking back to my Lord as I watched the birds drink the water they hadn't made, bathe in the water they hadn't prepared, dance in the water with their community. And my God said that He loved me; He would provide for me; I had value, and I would take one day at a time.

I spoke to God with gratitude. I apologized and asked Him for forgiveness for my sternness the morning before. I looked forward to meeting Him again tomorrow morning. To this day, this same God meets me every morning at four thirty and continues to bring scriptural guidance every time; He is faithful, He provides, and He always prays for me.

I showered and started packing, but then I wondered whether we had made any decisions the night before about traveling back to Southern California. I remembered discussion but no decision. But what I wanted was clear to me now. I knew that Frank had to drive his bike back to Southern California, and I suspected Stacey would use her plane ticket to fly home, so I thought: *Why don't I ride on the back of Frank's bike? He shouldn't be alone while traversing the same cement on which his friend, my husband, had passed.*

Once everyone had eaten breakfast, the discussion about transportation home ensued in earnest. They had seemed to have all the arrangements made, and then I dropped the bomb. I didn't want to ride in George's car; I wanted to ride with Frank on his bike. I wanted him to show me where Terry had died on the highway. I didn't think Frank should do this alone. Plus, I had all my gear. I trusted Frank as a driver. I felt peace. I thought Terry would have wanted me to do this. The table grew quiet as my words sank in.

Frank said, "You can't fall asleep on the back of my bike like you did when you were riding with Terry."

"Is that all you got?" I asked Frank.

"Yes, it is. I cannot lose both of you in one week."

"Then I will agree to that," I replied.

What wasn't spoken was that I didn't really care if I fell off the bike; I knew I would see God and my husband. I wasn't suicidal, but I also lacked the energy to live my life with adventure. Frank and I decided he would nudge me when we were near the area where my beloved had died just two days prior. We also decided I would stay on the bike until we needed gasoline, about ninety minutes after our departure. Then I was to sit in the car with George and my friends.

After about fifteen minutes of riding, Frank nudged my leg. I looked around and he pointed to an area on the road. I looked there, and my breath caught in my throat. He pointed to another area, and tears streamed down my face. I looked behind me and pointed at George's vehicle. Frank slowed down. I sat perfectly still with my hands on my legs, and my head dropped onto my chest.

I cried out to God in my heart, *Did you see him?* Gasping cries escaped from my mouth. *Did you try to help him?* More sobs. Deep breaths. *Did you come for him before he felt any pain? Oh God, please say "yes" to all my questions.*

Frank nudged my leg and asked if I wanted to stop. I looked into his eyes, saw his posture, and answered *no.* I knew it would kill us to relive those events. I don't regret my choice not to stop that day. Terry was never alone. We rode in silence for the next ninety minutes. After refueling, I got back on the bike. I needed to go the distance with Frank. I needed to be on the bike. I wasn't sure I could have handled the conversation in the car. Frank and I rode all twelve hours home together in silence. Our friends and family drove behind us, watching our every move—mile after mile.

We arrived at my home close to midnight. I opened my front door and completely lost it. The smell of my husband's cologne was right there at the front door! Our world together was evident everywhere I looked. His coffee mug was still in the sink. It would be harder than I thought to live in our home. I turned to my friends. Stacey and Frank immediately invited all of us to spend the night at their home. Wanda held me tight and told me they all understood. Where would I have been without friends? God was providing for my needs before I even realized it.

I didn't sleep long at Stacey and Frank's. At four thirty in the morning, I wandered out of bed and sat in their backyard near their fire pit. Their big dog, Nala, accompanied me. I was in a sweet yet darkening place: I felt no fear, no coldness, no thoughts—just numb and waiting for my God. It seemed like forever for Him to come to me. I went inside for a sweatshirt and socks, then went back outside and snuggled on the ground with Nala.

And then He came—not like before. There were no fountains or birds. No sense of anything spectacular. Just peace—breath-deeply-in-your-lungs peace. And the words in my head began to form: "And I will give you treasures hidden in the darkness—secret riches. I will do this so you may know that I am the LORD, the God of Israel, the one who calls you by name" (Isaiah 45:3). *Wow, Lord*, I prayed. *It's so dark where I am. I will have to trip over them, scrape my knee, and tumble deeper into the cave because I can't see a stinking thing. Are these really treasures? Are they secret riches? Because I can't see them. You hide things well.*

I laughed and then cried because I wanted those things deep in my heart. I wanted everything God had in mind for me except this. Death is not a treasure! Grief is not a treasure! This dark pit took my breath away. I was stumbling through life feeling blind. Silence. Then my heart was still enough to listen again: *These are treasures. You'll see, Linda ... someday ... no rush! I just want you to see me. I am your God. I know your name. You are not invisible to me! I see you ... and no matter how much you hurt, please know that I will never have you destroyed. I never promised you wouldn't hurt. I promised to never leave you, forsake you, or ever let you out of my gaze. You are mine! And I am all yours!*

It was Sunday morning and one of the first times in my ministry as a children's pastor that I didn't want to go to church. I didn't want to have to do something alone that Terry and I had done together. I didn't want to answer questions. I didn't want condolences. Truly, I just wanted to roll up into a ball and be invisible. The only thing that kept me going that week was knowing that my beloved Terry needed me to make the necessary funeral arrangements for him.

I'm so grateful that Tralee handled everything with the newspaper obituary and the slideshow of photographs. Wanda helped me select clothing from my and Terry's bedroom that was to be made into a quilt. The fabric was from Terry's favorite Harley destinations, and the concerts he enjoyed attending. My friend Lorraine made a beautiful, two-sided, T-shirt quilt that is still precious to me.

Frank made all of the arrangements for Terry's military burial at Riverside National Cemetery, which was to be held in October. The funeral home in Reno had shared a website with me where I could purchase my husband's urn.

The date for Terry's final burial was set to avoid my birthday (also in October) and to find a time when Wanda, her husband, and our godsons could attend. Stacey remained close to me. She kept me filled with hugs, food, and laughter.

She shared her home, her time, and her family with me. Terry's mom was struggling with the death of her only son who had survived Vietnam only to die in a traffic accident, and she was glad to see things were being taken care of.

Pastor David at Bay Hills Community Church was going to officiate Terry's celebration service the following Saturday, and Pastor Hous at Grace Lutheran Church was going to officiate Terry's celebration service the week after that. These plans were put into action on Sunday afternoon. George left to drive back by himself to Northern California to be with his family.

Monday came, and it was time to take my friend Wanda to the airport for her flight back to Northern California. I stopped at home to pick up some clothes, do a little laundry, and set a gauge for myself and my emotions. There, at the front door, were an assortment of flower-filled vases, baskets of greenery, balloons, and cards. I was a hot mess crying all over myself as I unlocked the door and walked into every room trying to find a place that didn't remind me of Terry. Of course, there was no such place. There was nowhere to hide!

I went outside to sit at our patio table, and memory after memory flooded my heart and mind. I walked to the mailbox that was already filled with notes, letters, and cards. Whew. There was nowhere to go that didn't remind me of him or my loss.

I laid on our bed and cried as I smelled his scent on the pillows. I held a picture frame of our wedding day against my chest. I know I had spoken the words *until death do us part,* but that was supposed to be when we were really old, and after we had spent many years together. It struck me that less than one week earlier we had been laughing together and preparing for our trip to Street Vibrations. I had no idea what the next week would hold for me.

Oh God, my mind and heart cried out again, *This hurts so badly. Can you just take me now? I don't want to hurt this badly! I don't want to live without him! I can't live without him! How will I even do this? How will I go back to work with kids at the church and school? They need someone who's filled with joy and life; they shouldn't see their pastor like this. How will I even make enough money to still be able to afford to live here? How can I possibly do this alone? I am your child; do you know how much this hurts me?*

I spent short amounts of time alone in my home. Terry's mom and I made final decisions for her son's celebration service. We would fly up to the Bay Area for the first of three services remembering Terry's life. My husband's ashes arrived at our home before I flew to Northern California. I wasn't sure how to handle them. My heart stopped, and I took in a huge breath. I sat down. As I opened the box, tears flooded my kitchen table.

How could a man larger than life, a man who said he would love me forever, a man whose presence still filled every corner of the home we shared—be contained in a box of ashes? The waves of grief continued to roll over me. If this was my reaction when I was alone with these ashes in my own home, how was I ever going to be able to make it through three services, listening to people share their memories of Terry? How would I speak with all of the people who would come to offer comfort and support?

Thankfully, the Lord had already given me what I needed during my time with Him that morning. Of course, I had no idea why the Lord had given me that verse until I was sitting at the table, sobbing and holding my husband's ashes. It was perfect. It was timely. It was meant for me that day, at that moment, at the kitchen table with all that was left of my husband's physical existence: "My health may fail, and my spirit may grow weak, but God remains the strength of my heart; he is mine forever" (Psalm 73:26). How grateful I was for God's perspective in the mornings. They became the standard with which I evaluated my emotions and decisions.

The celebration services went as planned. People came dressed in Harley attire as requested, and Harley riders and their bikes lined the parking lot. Most of my family, Terry's family, and people I hadn't seen for a long time attended—close to five hundred people in all. Stacey, Frank, and the kids sat with our family and held onto us. Tralee provided a beautiful pictorial tribute of his life set to the perfect music. Both services had worship teams, and my good friend Jay Strong sang Terry's favorite song, "I See the Lord." Jay sang with such emotion I felt as though he had taken us to heaven. The worship band sang with fervor.

Both services showed my video of thanks to those in

attendance, so I would not have to speak live. Both pastors delivered their heartfelt words and sermons. They also gave people time to share their memories. My goddaughter, Leslie, spoke profoundly at the first service of the promise Mr. Wonderful made to her to drive her to her wedding. Two of Terry's best friends, Jim and Terry, prayed and spoke at the beginning of the second service. All was going as planned at the second service until Pastor Hous asked me to come forward. This wasn't what we had talked about or what was in the order of the service. I had recorded a video message expressly so I would not have to say a word. I looked at him, first confused and then a little irritated. I was in no shape to speak to the congregation. Pastor Hous took a look at my face and addressed me by saying, "Linda, I know this isn't planned, but I believe God has told me to do this. Won't you please come stand here in the center with me?"

What was I to do? Be disrespectful to my pastor during my husband's funeral? That was not an option. Say no to God's leading? Double no. So I stood up from my seat, grabbed a ton of tissues, and patted my mother-in-law's hand. Taking a deep breath, I prayed my feet would support me as I walked to stand next to Pastor Hous. Once I made it successfully to his side, Pastor Hous began to explain God had never led him to do this before. He said he didn't know exactly what I was feeling—he couldn't, never having experienced any of my journey. He appealed to the widows and widowers sitting amongst us. I was one of their own pastors who needed their expertise.

Asking them to go back to "that day" when their lives were forever changed, he requested them to do a bold thing because God never wastes a moment or experience in our lives.

As they remembered "that day" in their own lives, he wanted them to join us up front and form a circle around me, so I could see them, and they could see me. In doing so, they offered physical evidence of their support. I could call them anytime, and they would help me navigate these new waters. Oh my goodness, I was undone. Men and women left their seats to hold me. They stood before me, beside me, and behind me. Pastor Hous prayed and asked the entire congregation to stand and pray for all of us. He asked them to extend their hands toward me.

It is possibly one of the top five moments of my entire life. Even though I was standing in front of a congregation of five hundred people, it felt strangely intimate. It was as if God was reaching down to little ole me through each person in that building. God was there for me. Who would think God would take the time for a four-foot, ten-inch widow with colorful hair like me?

I don't remember much of what happened after that. I was touched beyond words and no longer mad at my pastor. He had done the perfect thing because he obeyed God in that moment. During and after the service, my heart felt there was hope of renewal and refreshment. There was a community here to support me through this journey.

Our family could not stop crying, yet we felt peace those

afternoons, even as we met with friends, cried, listened, cried, hugged, and cried some more. After the services, the riders started their engines one by one to celebrate Terry's life. Every awesome set of loud pipes that rode past would forever serve as reminders of his life.

It's a process and a detour I never would have chosen, but God did. I see more clearly today because of it. The courses of our lives can change at any moment; our comfort zone can be ripped from our hearts. Hardships often prepare us for an unexpected journey; a journey in which we learn new perspectives on life that make us more responsive to and supportive of those around us.

Each road we travel has its own unique scenery. That's what life is like. Sometimes people walk with us for a season, and others continue with us throughout our entire journeys. After Terry's death, I knew each person walking beside me was a gift. I never came close to *liking* the road I had to travel to find these treasures, but God … Well, that's about all I can say.

But God, He gave me Himself, gave me hope, gave me His Word, and gave me people—personally and professionally. God gave me grace, breath, a desire to live, and safety to cry openly and unashamedly before Him. Let me encourage you today that the hard roads and detours you are walking on today are real, and they are hard … but God. Let God be your support as you walk through it all. Let God hold you and help you see the gifts around you. You are not alone.

NEW PERSPECTIVES

1. Are there others who are traveling a path similar to yours? How can you connect with them and support each other?

2. Examine the relationships you have with those in your life. Are any of them serving more as weight than support? What changes would need to take place for those relationships to become sources of support to you?

3. Examine the relationships in your life again. Are there any in which *you* are a weight more than a support? What would need to change for you to be more supportive?

4. Identify two or three pivotal, supportive relationships in your life. Take a few moments to pray for them, thanking God that He provided them to you and asking Him to bless them.

9

Aw, the People You Meet

WE ARE ALL CONNECTED

The heartfelt counsel of a friend
is as sweet as perfume and incense.

PROVERBS 27:9

*F*riendship takes us by the hand and reminds us that we are
not alone on the journey. I don't know if I would be here if
it hadn't been for the hands of many people in my life. Friends
hold us up; they support us as we share life's battles and victories, and they surround us when we cannot see. They help
guide us toward the next step. Sometimes they hold us as we
cry out in desperation, and sometimes they dance with us in
celebration.

It's not only friends and family who nurture and support
us but also professionals. Two years of grief counseling helped

me gain profound insight. During those dark days, I carried a piece of paper with me that listed the five most common signs of depression because I knew it was a slippery slope from grief to depression. Thankfully, Pastor Joe recognized I was sliding into depression, and he referred me to a grief counselor. My insurance wouldn't pay for these sessions, but I knew I needed it. Help comes in all forms. For me, my kitties gave me someone to love and hold.

I don't know how people walk through such dark and difficult pits without God. It was hard for me to process everything that had happened even with Him by my side. But God assists us with the relationships we already have or will have. Friends are a special help through that year full of firsts—the first birthday, the first wedding, the first Valentine's Day, the first night out with friends. My year of firsts included events I had already anticipated and a few surprises as well.

Terry died one month before my birthday, and by the time my birthday rolled around, I had planned and attended two celebration services on opposite ends of California and was preparing to bury Terry at the military cemetery two days after my birthday.

There is something to be said about the whirlwind of activity, tasks, and planning that happens immediately after a death—being surrounded by people, sorting through photographs, and capturing the experiences of a loved one's life into an obituary. It was a wonderful opportunity to feel the impact Terry had on each of our lives. The outpouring of understanding from people who tried to feel my pain and loss came even through practical needs, like making sure I was eating nutritious meals (which was the last thing on my mind) and helping me take care of some of life's daily responsibilities. Once the services were completed, however, life began to return to normal for everyone—everyone except me. My life was anything but normal.

Sleep was an elusive guest; either it didn't come, or it was all I could do. I avoided my bedroom because I would see Terry lying on the bed. I only slept in our bed when I was absolutely exhausted and confident I could handle it emotionally, but waking up next to an empty space was just as hard.

My appetite had changed, since I was now only cooking for one. Time … well, either the days went by in a flash or the moments dragged on. Relationships changed too. There was only one of me; I was not part of a couple. One chair at the table remained empty, and people struggled with what to say or not say at meals.

I wanted to return to normal as quickly as possible, but my heart and mind reminded me grief is a constant companion. So often we treat grief like an illness, like we're recovering from a cold or the flu. We are an optimistic species that tries and tries to conquer grief and attain the elusive "normal life." In my attempts to carry on, I would say *yes* to a lunch with friends but had to cancel thirty minutes beforehand because my resolve to be brave around others just wasn't strong enough yet.

Packing up his things was incredibly hard. His clothes in the closet smelled of him, and at times I even flung myself into them just to sense all of him that I possibly could. At times, I even told myself this was all a dream, and he would be home soon. These are the things you keep to yourself because people would otherwise think you needed time in a psychiatric unit.

Work filled up my days and nights, but tasks often took longer to complete because my mind and heart felt lost. The return to a semblance of routine was a step forward. I would set an alarm, take a shower, and work to bring structure back into my life. Some days were successful, but so many were not. On those days, it felt like I hadn't taken so much as a baby step forward. For me, the profound grace from my coworkers was a gift, and it gave me hope that someday I would be better; I would be stronger. I woke up every morning thinking, *Maybe it will happen today.*

At the school where I served, a young fifth grader gave me hope. He's an adult now, but I always tell him and his parents that he saved my life. His name is Shane. He and I had some "come-to-Jesus" meetings in my office for his behavior. We also had great times playing games and sharing life. We would speak in my windowed office with the shades open, yet it was private enough in there to speak freely. He came into my office in tears once, and we switched seats so no one would see him cry.

My birthday fell on a school day, and I was to speak in chapel. I shared the verse for that school year and explained how the verse was chosen the summer before (and before Terry died). The verse spoke about trusting God, who said that He would guide us along the best pathways for our lives. I don't remember the rest of the message I shared, but Shane approached me after chapel had finished and asked if he could come to my office for lunch. I used to have a sign-up sheet on my door to "reserve" lunch with me and four friends, but I had taken it down after the funeral because I didn't know which days I would feel "good enough" to talk, laugh, and eat lunch with them. I told Shane that it would be nice for us to do that together.

Two hours later, Shane was at my office door with his lunch. He asked if we could talk first. I sat in my normal spot next to the window, and we began to discuss the chapel message. He asked me if I ever questioned God about things.

"All the time," I answered. "God is big enough to hear me question, yell, and cry out to Him, and He still loves me."

Shane then asked about our verse, "Do you believe God picked out the death of Mr. Wonderful as the best pathway for you?"

"I believe God," I answered carefully, "but I really don't like that this is the best for me now. Maybe one day I'll recognize that, but not today."

Tears rolled down my face, and I bent over in half and cried. I felt a hand on my shoulder and looked up, and Shane was looking at me with tears in his eyes. I tried to stop because I didn't want to depress or scare him. I mumbled, "One day

I will know that God will use this, and I will see the best of this someday. I am sorry to disappoint you, Shane, but it's not today."

With the tenderness that only a child can possess, he said, "Pastor Linda, I think it would be good for us to switch chairs until lunchtime is over. I will sit in your chair, so that you can cry and nobody sees you. I will pray for you too, just like you did for me."

This is why I am a kid's pastor. This is how God heals us: with grace, love, and tenderness. Time spent crying unashamedly is a healing act. I have no idea how he prayed for me, but the next fifteen minutes were a wonderful example of God's lavish love to me. I was allowed to be broken in that moment without judgment. A child saved my life because God allowed Shane to be "Jesus with skin on" for me. Respite may not come from the places you expect, but look for them and receive them nonetheless. That day was a turning point for me to walk one step further in strength.

Another time I was blessed was while I met with our couples' small group. The members of the group took turns hosting the monthly dinner and choice of games, and Terry and I were supposed to host the upcoming month. I couldn't imagine preparing a meal, setting the table, and sitting down to eat because the only thing my mind could focus on was his empty chair. I called the wives and said I couldn't cook the dinner and thought it best I leave the group. I was no longer a wife or part of a couple, so I tried to graciously bow out.

They didn't let me go. Instead, they improvised. We met at a restaurant to watch the World Series together, and we adapted. I eventually left the couples' group by replacing myself with another couple, but the relationships I had forged when I was in that group remain to this day. We have all stayed connected as we go through life together, and I am thankful for their fierce and relentless love for me throughout my hardest and darkest seasons.

I stayed home alone on Thanksgiving, my wedding anniversary, and Christmas Day. I called my mom and told her I couldn't be around people this year; it just hurt too much. I worked the Christmas Eve services at our church—all seven of them, and I spent most of the early morning of Christmas Eve helping my friends, Terri and David, put their kids' toys and presents together.

It was a tradition for Terry and I to present Jesus a birthday gift on Christmas morning before we opened our presents from each other. I had taken out the little boxes we used for our gifts and set them on the fireplace mantle earlier in the week. I prepared a fire and sat on the floor in front of it in tears. I told the Lord He already had my birthday gift to Him: He had Terry. In my mind, I distinctly heard the words, *You never gave him to me. His time was done, so he is here singing "Happy Birthday" to me in person. I just took the birthday gift he gave me last year.*

I sat up and grabbed both boxes then sat back down to read the gifts we had given Jesus the Christmas before. Terry's paper read, "Lord, I give you my desire to be so intimate with you that I could just touch you in this coming year." I cried out to God loudly, "His death is not what he meant! He meant something else!" My body began to shake and heave. Deep wails I had never heard came out of my body. I don't know how long I sat there and cried, and then there was peace.

But God wasn't done with our conversation. As quietly as God spoke to me regarding Terry's box, the Lord gently said, *Do you remember your gift to me? I took that gift also.* I did remember. I opened the box, and there was my handwriting: "Happy birthday, Jesus. I give you my desire to know you more desperately than I ever have in my life. Can you make me more desperate for you as my only place I go to in life? I want to want you more than I have at any other time." Yep, the Lord took that gift as well.

In tears, I asked the Lord, "What can I give you now? I have nothing to give you except for my broken heart. I can't think of anything else I can do or say or give to you except for that."

And softly, I heard the Lord reply, *That's perfect. I will take your broken heart. I will take whatever you give me, and I promise I will take good care of your heart. It is the perfect gift because you are giving me all the pieces, and I treasure each one of them because I treasure you.*

In that moment, God reminded me of the passage in Psalm 34:18: "The LORD is close to the brokenhearted; he rescues those whose spirits are crushed." It was confirmation that the

Lord knew where I was, knew what I brought to Him, and that He promised me His presence and hope. The verse reminded me that I had value even though I was no longer part of a couple or a wife, and despite the brokenness I felt, the Lord would not toss me aside. I felt crushed to the very core of who I was and thought I had finally reached the bottom of my grief.

But I was going to sink deeper. The holidays were killing me. Thankful for the care and concern of my friends, I was now becoming a little more hurt, angry, and not very happy with the holiday season. I called all my friends, wished them an awesome time of gathering with family and friends this upcoming New Year, and let them know I changed the locks. No need for a suicide watch; I just needed time to myself in my home. I had just posted a "For Sale" sign, and I wanted to grieve yet another loss. I begged God that night not to let the clocks move forward. I didn't want to leave Mr. Wonderful in 2006 and move into 2007 without him.

New Year's Eve was especially difficult. I sat by the fire and watched the ball drop on television in country after country and felt my heart sink deeper and deeper. I hardly ate. I cried, I wailed, and I held my kitties—days and nights passed. On the third day in January, I had a scary realization that I was quickly moving from grief into depression. I hadn't showered for three days; that was significant. I hadn't had anything to eat or drink for two days. I had turned off my phone and never answered the knocks at my door except to call out, "I'm fine, please go home. I will call soon. I am not done here." I pulled out my sheet of paper showing the signs of depression and knew I needed counseling, and I needed it fast. I didn't know how I could walk through the new year; I just knew that I would. The advice from my grief counselor helped me build a solid foundation for working through the many waves of emotion that comes with grief.

People had helped me from the moment of Terry's death: the funeral arrangements, my birthday, Thanksgiving, our anniversary, Christmas Eve, Christmas Day, and a scary New Year's Eve. God had covered and prepared me and others for this. It was now the new year and a new list of firsts—Terry's birthday in early February, Valentine's Day when I found all the cards we had exchanged throughout our years of marriage. I displayed them after my grief counselor verified that was okay.

My house sold three weeks before Palm Sunday. Parents and staff from the school and church packed my entire belongings into my new cave near Long Beach. I had decided not to put anything into storage. I threw out every flower vase since I would never receive flowers again. That was hard. As a widow, I had to sift through my life and take with me only the things I considered important. How thankful I am for the people who packed and stored my favorite purple couch and chair, who saved and stored my china, who packed, moved, and cleaned both our home and my new cave. I loved my little one-bedroom place near the beach. I didn't see many sunsets since I often worked late to save myself from long evenings alone;

the sunsets I did see were incredible. I still couldn't sleep much and learned that sunrises filled me with hope for another day to learn how to do life again. I took a gazillion pictures on my phone so that throughout each day when my life seemed dark, I could remind myself of God's faithfulness on a new day.

Probably the hardest thing that my counselor asked me to do was remove my wedding rings from my hand. I was appalled. I had seen most widows and widowers have their rings on or wear them on a chain around their neck. Why would my counselor ask me to do such a thing? By now, I'm sure it comes as no surprise to you that I challenged him and asked him why. He simply answered the question with a question, "Why do you wear them?"

I answered, "They remind me of our love—my love for him and his love for me. They remind me I am still his."

"Really? Isn't that a bit dishonest?" my counselor asked.

My jaw dropped open wide. Stunned, I wondered if my counselor had lost his mind. I answered loudly and firmly, "Not at all."

He waited a few moments, then moved his chair closer to me and gently said, "Linda, in watching you preach and lead a kid's ministry in both church and school, I have learned that your highest value in life, in God, in others, and yourself is truth." And pointing to my ring, he said, "This does not display truth. Would you think about that for a minute?"

Oh, the tears began to flow. I looked at my rings. Terry and I had designed these rings ourselves. They were as unique as our relationship had been. I remembered our engagement. I remembered his eyes, his love, and now he was gone. This would be wrong, wouldn't it? I was afraid in that moment I would forget him and us, and my rings were the most tangible reminder of our marriage.

I asked my counselor a slew of questions: "How do I do this? How could I do this? Why should I do this? Why does everything have to be harder on me than on everybody else? This is just not fair, and I just can't—won't—do this." We were at the end of our session, and we closed in prayer and exchanged polite goodbyes.

The drive home was horrendous. The traffic and my struggling heart made it feel even longer and harder. I went directly home, watched a sunset, and cried once again. I was all alone in a new location. It had to be the greater part of a year since Terry's death, and now I didn't know whether to take up my counselor's suggestions or not. I had no enlightenment, no God conversations, just another shard of my broken heart stabbing me in the chest (so dramatic, huh?).

I went inside to shower and took off my jewelry and rings as I usually did. After I was dressed, as I hung up my towel, it hit the box that held Terry's rings and jewelry. It fell off the shelf and onto the floor. The impact forced the box open, and his rings spilled out. I fell to the floor, curled up in the fetal position, and began to cry. I picked up his rings and felt undone for three hours. My heart felt newly broken. Any healing that had occurred over the past eight months was now void. My heart was bleeding out, and I couldn't catch my breath; I hurt so much I didn't feel the pain.

I knew in that moment something had to be done. I had to fix this. I needed God to give me options since I had cut off my counselor that day. "Dear God," I cried out. "What can I do? What should I do? How do I do this? My counselor said I needed to take my wedding rings off, but he didn't say anything about Terry's. I don't think I can live in fear. I can't be afraid of his rings and allow my heart to rip open again. These rings are no longer life-giving; these rings tell me what was … How can I live today if I stay in the past? I don't ever want to forget, Lord. I just don't want to ever forget."

As I waited desperately for God to answer, a thought began to form: an option, a solution. It wasn't one I had ever heard or read; this idea was something new. I picked up both rings and held them tightly in my hands. I remembered the gift of love, adventure, and marriage that was given to me. But I knew what I needed to do the next day. I placed both of our rings in his jewelry box and put the box in my purse. I never put that wedding ring on again, and I slept peacefully that night. I slept so soundly I missed the sunrise the next morning.

I went to work and kept the jewelry box in the trunk. I wondered if I would change my mind, but I didn't. I went to a jeweler a friend had referred me to, and I introduced myself and my ideas for the rings. He listened, and then we designed something new. I told him I was going out of town for two weeks, and I would like the two new designs ready when I returned. He understood how reluctant I was to give the rings to him. Goodbyes are always hard—especially when you have to repeat them again and again.

Two weeks later, I returned and made an appointment to pick up the new design with my friend Rachel. I wasn't sure how I would feel or react, and I wanted—needed her support. Let me tell you about the miracle of God and what I designed. The first piece wasn't hard: It had been a gold ring with a brownish gold, snake-eye gem. I had redesigned it as a pendant, and all of the gold was molded into an elongated teardrop, and the gem was set inside and near the bottom. My heart was lightened. I wasn't sad; it was actually pretty cool.

The second piece was made from our wedding rings. Because my husband was a Vietnam veteran and I was a cancer survivor, the platinum and white gold from our rings was used to form a ribbon for a pendant. My center stone was at the top of the ribbon, and his center stone was below it. We took all the baguettes from my ring and filled in the ribbon with enough of them to signify every year of love we had shared.

You see, God made something new out of each memory. The metal and the diamond signified what we were, but it also combined those elements into something new. It wasn't a shrine or even a remembrance. It was a new creation—something to be celebrated. Rachel said she watched and waited for the tears and the sadness, but I can honestly say it was not sad. The experience told me that God never wastes a moment, a love, a loss, a hurt, or a pain without using it. I put on the pendant that day. People still comment on it not knowing its story. It is something beautiful to behold and enjoy and celebrate.

I had a great time at my next appointment with my counselor. I wore my new design, my new creation. I was a woman filled with hope that God was doing the same in me. My counselor was very impressed with the design and all that it meant to me. It was a tangible reminder of the work God had done in my heart.

The summer continued as I sought the Lord and the work he had for me now. I sensed He was doing something, and I moved back to the Bay Area before the first anniversary of Terry's homegoing. I wanted to be closer to my mom and support her throughout her unpredictable health challenges. This called for a trip to Street Vibrations in Reno on Terry's repaired bike. George had bought the bike to keep it in the family, and he traveled with me to the event. When I returned to the Bay Area, my year of firsts was over, which I had decided as my marker for when things should be "normal" again, but the darkness continued and seemed to intensify. For many, the second year can be even harder. I needed to continue in counseling.

Learning a new normal, as my counselor called it, can be described best as the need for me to learn to deal with situations like holidays rather than lament what was or could have been. This process is something that has to be done after any dramatic life change. When Christmas came that second year, I told my friends I wouldn't be buying or decorating a tree. That didn't sit well with them. I had been gone for a few days, and when I returned and walked into my home, I was greeted by a tree they had bought and decorated. I was so ungrateful and felt they violated my space (and I told them so). Part of my reasoning for not wanting to decorate was because I couldn't bring myself to even open our ornaments; it was too hard and there were too many memories.

The next year, I lived my new normal and invited all of my godchildren and their parents for a dinner, and I decorated a tree with simple decorations (but still without ornaments because ornaments meant sentimentality). The following year, I added more to my new normal with five ornaments from our life. It was a process for sure, but the healing had started. My heart was healing from the blessing and reality of the gift of marriage I had been given.

The pain and the terrible toll of fear, anger, confusion, and uncertainty that happens when our world collapses around us can often seem more than we can bear. Things that used to matter no longer make much difference. An unexpected, or even expected death is a stressful experience. Breakups and divorces can leave us wide open and vulnerable to deep wounds. Many times, we are so tied to one another that we don't know where our significant other ends and where we begin.

Please seek counseling for help to process such radical changes in your life. I didn't know how to navigate these new waters, so I found a grief counselor who did. At times, I felt as though I was drowning, and I didn't know how to resuscitate myself. New beginnings aren't easy, and they cannot start until the ending has been dealt with properly.

Your professional counselor may come from your health plan or your pastor. Let him or her offer new perspectives on what you're going through. Be honest and open to those closest to you. Listen to what they say. Establish new priorities, read books, exercise, and volunteer in your church and community. Bring new friends into your community. It can be a wild roller-coaster ride, but realize you are on it and you are not alone.

Here is one last story I would like to leave with you—not a complimentary one, but an honest account of a tough season in my life during the year I learned my new normal. I call this episode "The Kitchen Table Bible-Waving Rant." Sadly, I must admit that even after all the ways my friends, family, and God tended to my attempts at moving forward and out of the dark pit, my soul was still in a state of unrest. I wasn't complete. I still longed for my old life, when I was married and walking happily and expectantly into our future together. Somehow, I felt I had one foot in today's reality, and the other foot still firmly planted in the past. I kept walking toward what was in front of me (limping really), but I knew I would one day have to face the past with God decisively. And that day came.

I came home from my mom's church service on Good Friday with my Bible in hand, and I began to feel agitated. I moved to put my Bible on my nightstand, and it opened to the very promise I have held God to since the beginning of this horrendous journey. The passage was Psalm 30:11–12: "You did it: you changed wild lament into whirling dance; You ripped off my black mourning band and decked me with wildflowers. I'm about to burst with song; I can't keep quiet about you. GOD, my God, I can't thank you enough" (MSG).

I didn't feel this way at all. The transition from mourning to dancing was a promise I had been waiting for ... and now it was in my face. God had not kept His Word, and I felt that I needed to remind Him that I was nowhere close to dancing. So I did what every sane woman would do: I stormed into my kitchen with the Bible open and hanging beside my right leg. I pushed out a chair from my kitchen table, stood on it, and looked up to my cathedral ceiling. I needed to get higher so God could see and hear me—crazy, huh?

I slammed one foot on the table and then the other one. I waved my Bible in the air and into the very face of God and cried out, "You promised … You promised. How long before you will keep your Word? I can't even hear the music, let alone dance and sing any praise to you in gratefulness. … And I can't dance alone—it's not in me."

Then I sensed His tender Spirit. I felt my heart break again, and I knew the time would come, but not tonight. I actually received a gift from God called hope. I felt heard, and I scrambled down the table quickly as I realized just who I was talking to. I sat under the table just in case lightning struck. I laughed at myself, knowing full well God gives me the freedom to speak. He longs to speak to us. He longs to share His thoughts and reasonings, but I don't think we wait long enough for Him to do so. I imagine God listening to our thoughts, prayers, and cries, and He gets ready to answer us, but we get up and leave. We don't allow Him time to speak to our hearts. That night under the table, I let Him hold me in His arms. Although I never heard Him give me a date for when His promise would be fulfilled, I knew He was faithful to His Word. I knew He was faithful to me.

My kitchen became the place where I meet Him. And no, I have never climbed back on that table, but I have often met Him under the table. It is still that private place where I know God met me and will meet me again. I am reminded of His tenderness in caring for my heart under there. He met this crazed woman who just wanted answers. Although none came, He came.

Maybe today you are in a desperate place like I was. God

desires to meet us wherever we are. He knows us before we are made. He counts every hair on our heads. He is crazy for you. You don't need to jump through any special hoops or make promises you may or may not keep. Just come as you are—broken, desperate, in need of Him ... it doesn't matter to Him. He just wants you like crazy.

NEW PERSPECTIVES

1. What promises or dreams are you still waiting for?
2. Have you shared those promises and dreams with a counselor or a friend? Are you waiting for God to answer?
3. Have you stayed long enough in His presence to hear an answer, or have you left too quickly?
4. Take ten minutes to yourself right now. Go outdoors and ask Him your questions. Then wait for an answer.
5. Repeat this again before you go to bed. In quietness, open your heart for God to speak to you.

10

Showering Off the Day's Ride

REFLECTION IS LIFE-CHANGING

Everything in life should
be done with reflection.

JOHN ADAMS

*I*t has been said that the two most important things a great
leader needs to make a decision are adequate rest and the
ability to reflect and remember past events. Both abilities shift
perspective to the forefront of our consciousness.

After a long ride, Terry and I were strategic about where
we stayed for the night and where we could walk to get dinner.
You see, although I loved the ride, I loved the shower that came
at the end of the day's ride; it etched the day's events into my
memory. I could enjoy the warmth of the water, the refreshing
scent of my shower gel, and just stand there (usually smiling),

recalling the day. The smells, the beauty, the spectacular mountains, the sandy beaches beside lakes, streams, or oceans—and sharing this time with my husband, my co-adventurer. He showed me the joy in stopping our ride whenever we spotted two to three cars stopped alongside the highway; he saw potential for an unseen adventure!

I enjoyed our walks to dinner after a long day of riding because our bodies often felt stiff after sitting in a straddle position for so long. The freedom to take our time on these long rides and be totally present in our environment—with our thoughts and with each other—was an amazing gift. We weren't caught up on our phones or computers. We just took everything in, gulp after gulp.

Dinner was often filled with animated conversation: "Remember when we nearly ran out of fuel? Did you see that deer cross the stream with her babies?"

Terry usually responded to my observations with a version of, "No, somebody had to be driving the motorcycle." Or he would ask, "Is there any place you would have rather been today?" After dinner, we didn't spend much time watching television. We just rolled into each other's arms—exhausted and content. That was the best way we could get ready for the next day's adventure.

When I think about the day of Terry's death, I can't help but think that God had already prepared me and my heart with backstories that let me see His hand in that one day that changed me forever. And when I think He already had all of my backstories in place for that day, I know He has arranged all of my days yet to come.

Oh, I have lots of backstories, but I am just going to share a few. You see, God has orchestrated your lives also. He has paved the way with tons of preparation. In no way am I promising you'll like all of it! You will never hear me say how happy and blessed I am that the Lord took Mr. Wonderful home to be with Him. I will say, however, that I can see His hand; He provided community around me, He gave me enough for each day's challenges, and He orchestrated everything around me in preparation for the day's events. I adore the dependence and intimacy that I share with God.

I don't *like* the way He did it. I didn't like how long I stayed in the dark pit of grief either. But I am so thankful He never deserted me, even when He seemed very quiet for a while. He provided profound and wise counsel to me. He gave me friends who I will have for life—despite the ways my pain often made me behave like a brat toward them. My service as a pastor didn't give me any privilege or advantage in coping. The only privilege I have, which also belongs to you, is that He seeks us out. He is our Father, our Daddy, our Provider, our Protector, our Comfort, our Wonderful Counselor, our Guide, our Healer, and our Hiding Place.

Backstory #1: Last Talk with Mr. Wonderful

I had spoken at a women's retreat over the weekend and came home dehydrated on Sunday. I had headaches and felt tired, but my heart was full. The retreat had been a wonderful time of sharing, crying, laughing, and little sleep. Terry and I would be leaving for the motorcycle event in Reno at six in the morning on Thursday, so I contacted my doctor on Monday and told her my symptoms. She met me in the emergency room and administered some fluids. As I was in the emergency room being seen by my doctor, I could hear a guest on the *Oprah Winfrey Show* talking about a book he had written about the importance of paying attention to the language of the dying. I was intrigued, so I listened.

Hmm, I thought as I listened, *maybe that explains why some people who are dying repeatedly ask to see a specific person and seem to hang on until that person arrives. It may also explain the wisdom spoken in those last few moments of a person's life. Rather than fussing with the details and the dying person's need for comfort, maybe the best thing to do is listen to them.*

The author said he had watched people finally forgive themselves for past offenses because the dying person seemed to set them free with their words. He also mentioned that a person's last words can be the balm that our souls need to find peace after a loved one passes. Of course, sometimes we're unaware a person's words are their last, but I filed away this author's wisdom in my brain anyway. As a pastor, I thought his message would prove to be sound advice I could offer to grieving families and friends. His message seemed life-giving to me. And, then, just like that, I was released from the emergency room and went home.

Fast-forward to the last words Terry spoke to me on the

telephone just days after leaving the hospital. I had called him at the airport during my layover although this call was not something we had planned. I took a chance anyway, and I rejoiced at the sound of his voice when he picked up. Since the call hadn't been arranged, I listened that much more intently.

I thank God for the words Terry first spoke on that call about him "almost being home." Of course, I was thinking he was referring to something that might have happened on the road and caused him to turn back to our home in Southern California, but he corrected that quickly. Now I realize he was "almost home" with his God. It will always bring tears to my eyes, but what better place could I wish for him to be?

The next comment he made was his amazement at how far he had traveled those five hundred plus miles without me. This was significant because together we had put 98 percent of those miles on that Harley. His words of amazement still bring me comfort and a sense of gratitude for having had the kind of marriage that provided us with such companionship and adventure. Hours later, it would be profoundly clear to me that my next miles would be without him, but I am forever grateful that God spared me from having to watch him die that afternoon on the highway.

The final comment Terry made was of a surprise that awaited me upon my arrival in the Reno airport. The surprise was not the one I would ever wish for myself or any of you reading this. It was nothing I imagined that surprise to look like. He didn't arrive at the airport with his signature grin to pick me up with excitement and anticipation for the weekend's events. In fact, he wasn't even at the hotel. As minutes passed and updates started to come in, I still waited for the surprise. I expected a surprise I would take delight in, not one I would wail through. After many, many months, God restored my desire to approach surprises with anticipation and enthusiasm. I began to relearn the gift of hope that sits before all of us.

I still carry Terry's last words deep within my heart, and I'm grateful for them. Perhaps you can take a moment and reflect on your own life with gratitude—whether that's challenging or easy. Gratitude is the key to remembering. Build an attitude of gratitude. Small steps are okay, but try something new today.

Backstory #2: Frank's Lost Phone

A few days before the accident, God was not only busy orchestrating events in my life, but also in the life of Mr. Wonderful's dear friend and companion, Frank, who was on the ride with him to Reno. Frank had lost his phone, but his life and work required him to have one. He lost all of his contacts when he lost his phone, and when his phone was replaced, he imported his wife's contacts to his phone. He used her friends and family as a starting place for accumulating his contact list again. It was because of the inconvenience of losing his phone that he even had Pastor Hous' cell phone number. It had been imported from Stacey's phone as Pastor Hous was a patient at her dental practice. Pastor Hous' contact information was listed right beneath Frank's home number in his contact list.

After my late husband was pronounced dead on Highway 80, Frank needed to speak with someone. Of course, I was in the air with his wife traveling to Reno, so he couldn't contact either of us. He didn't have any other contacts for our family. Frank opened his phone to call Stacey's grandma, but then he saw Pastor Hous' number and pressed send. It had been thirty minutes since Terry died, and our pastor was with friends who directed Frank to a pastoral couple who lived nearby in Lake Tahoe. The couple was to meet me at the hotel and tell me of Terry's death, while Frank attended to the details at the scene of the accident. Terry's mom, Patsy, lived minutes from where Pastor Hous was in Huntington Beach, and Pastor Hous remained with Patsy while the couple from Lake Tahoe notified us in our hotel room in Reno.

When I think of these details, I am amazed at how meticulous our God is in the details of our lives (and deaths). Who would have thought that Frank's lost phone would implicate God's tenderness in the way he touches everyone involved in this tragedy? Look for the God-touches in your life. You may be surprised how intimately He is involved with you. The people you meet, the work activities around you, or maybe the simple kindness of the cashier at your supermarket. You are special enough for God to be so involved with you. Please remember how crazy in love He is with you.

Backstory #3: God Knows Our Every Need

I received a call from my doctor at six o'clock in the evening prior to my departure for Reno. Terry and I were in the midst of packing our things into the Harley's saddlebags and preparing to pull out of our driveway in twelve hours. What could she possibly want to talk about? She had only two things to say: "Linda, I have been praying for you. I believe the Lord has asked me to call you in the middle of your packing," and "Can you see if you can board the plane with your girlfriend who's flying to Reno? I mean, you've already seen these five hundred miles of cement, and I know you don't like repeating roads you've been on before. It would give you one more day of rest to recover from the busyness of the women's retreat. Since you have ten days of riding ahead of you, would you consider flying instead?"

After our call, I chatted with Terry, and he agreed it was a wise call. I booked the same flight as Stacey and secured a ride to the airport. I left my clothes on the bike in the saddlebags, the only thing that would be different was that I would wave goodbye to Terry instead of sitting behind him on our bike.

Minutes before Terry's accident, he and Frank had stopped to stretch their legs and get a cold drink from a gas station near the border of California and Nevada. As they resumed their travels, both bikes entered onto the highway in the slower lane. Frank stayed in this lane, but Terry moved into the fast lane. The slower lane had fresh blacktop on it and was higher than the grated road in the fast lane. Terry's bike started to wobble, but it looked like he was getting a hold of it. Then, he was suddenly ejected from the bike and his body landed on the pavement of the slow lane where he was hit by a camper and then an eighteen-wheeler truck.

I believe God kept me from riding that day to avoid this disaster. I never saw any of it, but Frank did (and still does). Frank slowed his bike and came alongside my husband's body on the highway. Other Harley riders stopped the traffic on both sides of the highway, and every vehicle was at a standstill. Terry was not alone. Frank, his firefighting buddy, was beside him and equipped to handle emergencies. Emergency vehicles were everywhere. Terry was pronounced dead at the very same time my plane took off from San Jose. Two months after the accident, I read the coroner's report and saw the photographs of his body covered on the side of the road that had visible skid marks and showed where his body had been dragged for a bit.

Jeremiah 29:11 was quoted a lot to me in those first few weeks. I understand that people just don't know what to say sometimes, and maybe people wanted to offer me comfort through God's Word since I was a pastor. But I started to get a bit edgy about this passage. The verse states: "'For I know the plans I have for you, says the LORD. 'They are plans for good and not for disaster, to give you a future and a hope.'"

First, let me say that I believe every word of the Bible is breathed by God. Sometimes, however, verses are taken out of context. And yet, I knew in my head and my heart that God did and does have a plan for me. And as I noted earlier in the book, God doesn't always ask our permission to choose the plan for us. What I have walked through is a not plan I would have chosen, and this verse bothered me. I didn't see the good, and I certainly wasn't feeling peace. These plans were supposed to give me a future and a hope? Well, I didn't see any of that either. If I had been on that bike and watched my husband die, I would have prayed for my own death. I can honestly tell you that for months following his death, I wasn't suicidal, but my attitude was "If I die, then oh well."

But there were two words in this verse that intrigued me: God's plans are for peace and not for *disaster* or *destruction*. Some translations use the word *harm*. Well, I read my Hebrew Bible, biblical commentaries, and Bible studies to understand the definition of the word *harm*. It is translated well here as *disaster*. Jeremiah 29:11 is not reassuring because it means God will shower us with only success and blessings in life; rather, it is reassuring because it means that God has a purpose for our suffering. He never promised for me to escape hurt, and whew, I hurt for a long time.

God protected me from destruction that day. He comforted me in my pit of despair. He must have collected countless bottles of my tears from days, weeks, and months of crying. So many of my friends had their own grief. They stood with me. I tried to be brave and strong, but I often ran away. We encouraged each other and cried and held one another as life was returning to normal for many of them, but I was still lost. I felt lost, even with God. Yet again, God would restore breath into my lungs bit by bit. The kids at school had silly jokes and riddles to tell me, and the sunsets over the beach in my new cave filled me with enough hope to make it through the night.

Suffering is part of the living process, but we don't have to suffer alone. God is there. Friends and family are there. Good, wise, and professional counseling is readily available. Make good choices and keep smart people around you. When you do everything you can do, God will step in and do what you cannot. Sometimes the hardest thing to do is learn to love yourself.

Each day I make a choice: I choose joy. God already knows what today will bring, and He is planning all the backstories. Choosing your attitude will change your perspective. I love that He has plans for me; He has my back, but He also has my present and my future. Please don't ever give up. Cling to those around you and walk these journeys together. God has a purpose and a reason for your struggles. He gives us the gift of His faithfulness. And He never wastes a moment, experience, emotion, or choice—good or bad. He longs to make all things new.

We are connected and never alone. But sometimes, the love of God and the faithfulness of His promises require great patience on our part. I wish I could say I always waited patiently. Through it all, God is in control and will never fail us, harm us, or destroy us. And if you are not part of His family today, then I am praying that you may know Him and ask Him to help you depend on Him, His paths, and His choices.

God's timing is sometimes way different than yours or mine. When I turn around and look at things from His perspective, *sometimes* what I have walked through makes much more sense (but not always). He was there for me when my world collapsed and the bottom seemed to have fallen away. And the reality is that He is there for you too.

NEW PERSPECTIVES

1. God prepares all of our days.
2. God never wastes an experience.
3. The power of choice comes in the arena of attitude.
4. Remembrances and reflections are powerful.
5. Look inside, but move on quickly to looking outside and up to God.
6. Take new steps of faith and adventure.

11

It's All about the Journey, Not the Destination

WHERE WE'VE BEEN AND WHERE WE'RE GOING

I am prepared to go anywhere,
provided it be forward.

DAVID LIVINGSTONE

C. S. Lewis, one of my favorite authors, once said, "Hardships often prepare ordinary people for an extraordinary destiny." The quote doesn't say I am extraordinary; in fact, I am quite ordinary. But the thought that I could have an extraordinary destiny excites me. It makes me think that all I have walked through was not wasted; it matters. I serve an extraordinary God who is above ordinary and who gives me hope.

My love for adventure began when I was quite young, and

even now I am still in love with what is ahead. There are so many possibilities to explore! How about you? Are you in love with the adventure God has prepared for you? Are you excited about the purpose and destiny that God has for you? He won't waste any of your suffering or experiences you've had.

Embracing the plans God has for me—even the suffering and challenges—is quite a departure from the woman I have shared with you over these previous pages. My hope for you is that you will see how your challenges can change you. Let me encourage you: No matter how many positive attitudes and well-intentioned resolves you make, forward progress is all about taking baby steps. I remember times when I agreed to lunch with a team member, friend, or even church member at nine in the morning but would call and cancel by eleven thirty. I have great friends who are also quite creative—they learned to show up about the time I normally would call them to bail, and they waited for me. Good push. Great strategy. And we usually had a great time, which helped me build confidence that I could move along on my journey and not drown in my pool of tears.

It's important for us to recognize that we're all on a journey. We may not have the same journeys, but our stories are sometimes similar. Some of our emotions and reactions are alike. God gives us hope to dream again with a renewed spirit and strength to continue walking upright. I wish I could tell you when you'll see that change come, but it's different for each and every one of us. But I'm here to tell you that change will come! Look for it! You will experience a glimmer of hope, a deeper breath than you thought possible, and fewer tears today than there were yesterday. But if I could leave you with a profound thought that has proved phenomenally helpful to me, it would be this: *All* of my journeys make me ready for today. Yep, even those challenging, flat-out hard ones I *never* wanted to experience have prepared me for today.

One person shared with me that after winter always comes spring, but our calendars may be different. I took that concept literally since Terry died in September. I remember watching leaves change and bottling up my emotions that season, although I cried a tear for every leaf that fell off the trees and bushes around my house. Then came winter. I felt shut off from the world. I was always cold in my soul. I felt like a seed deep beneath the soil that desired nothing more than to touch the warm, summer sun. The days were shorter and the nights longer, which made everything seem even more dark and depressing. It felt like I was living the longest night every day of my life. I did not want to be in that place!

I am usually an upbeat, positive person, but I had no one ahead of me on this journey and no gauge for what to expect. I thought something must be wrong since I couldn't seem to crawl out of this dark pit. I asked myself questions like, *Am I normal? Does it really take this long? Shouldn't I be displaying God's strength and joy and just go about my new life?* I asked because, in all honesty, I wasn't anywhere near that place (wherever that place was). I wasn't sure where I could or should go to learn how to thrive again after such a profound loss.

I am so thankful for online retailers. I ordered every self-help book I thought might help. I went to a Christian counselor, ordered daily devotional emails that pointed me to Christ, got out of bed, didn't drink myself to oblivion, showered, changed my clothes, and went outside for at least sixty minutes every day. My soul was hurt, and my spirit crushed; I was brokenhearted, and I felt like the cold dampness of winter was taking up residence within my bones. But even amid all this, I learned I could not rush time or the grieving process. I couldn't beckon a new season in my heart any easier than I could the pages of the winter months from a calendar.

How I longed for spring to take flight in my heart. If I could have made the plants bloom faster, the rain to stop, the lightness to shine on my dreary soul, I would have. My spring didn't come on time even according to the calendar. Winter days felt like recurring death, but spring signified the promise of new life. Death would be overcome! I could walk and perhaps even run again. The direction didn't matter; my soul wanted to live. But once again the tears would appear. I brushed them aside and told myself that at least I *wanted* to live. I couldn't see that I was living in my past—a past that included death, loss, and heartache.

Spring became my focus! Our home was sold, and I was to move the day after Palm Sunday. I was so ready. I vigorously packed boxes with friends because I thought my life was going to suddenly return. Life was going to look different—this I knew; I just wasn't sure what "different" would look like. Anything was better than the doldrums of winter.

Preaching Palm Sunday was my joy; God was going to rescue me! He would walk triumphantly into my daily life as He walked into Jerusalem so many years before. I would certainly be like one of those people who was excited for the King to enter their home and country to overthrow anything before them. Yep, this would be me!

I could almost taste it. I wanted God to come into my receptive heart, make all things new, and bring home the victory of the One who performed miracles. He could feed me, protect me, heal me to walk and see, raise the dead, teach me, love me, and take away my broken heart! I wanted him to be present with me now. I had thought death was hard, but I came to learn that living was so much harder. I felt more and more like a shell of a person who was being emptied from the inside. I cried out for spring with hope. Spring is coming! Spring will come!

In anticipation, I woke up Palm Sunday ready to preach about the thing I wanted in my life: the surprise of Jesus coming triumphantly as King. I preached at all four services, and Jesus didn't rescue me. I waited alone between services and went home that afternoon and cried out again for a new chapter of my life in my small, 750-square-foot bungalow. I resolved that if this was the path I was to walk, then I would do it well. I would choose to embrace what God had for me in this season of spring.

Yet the despondent, grieving woman inside of me would not give up. *Maybe*, I thought, *I have to wait until the end of spring.* I unpacked on Good Friday and attended services that afternoon and evening. I finished unpacking on Saturday and offered to serve all five services Sunday morning and afternoon. How often I looked at the decorated cross alive with vibrant-colored flowers—no longer shrouded in a black curtain. I prayed for that resurrection of life in me: to breathe deeply once again.

I prayed Christ would come alive in me—that He would call my name like He did for Mary in the garden. She was searching for Him, but He was not in the grave. He was gone, and she was weeping. And through her tears, she didn't know it was Christ until He spoke her name. As I thought about the story of Mary, my heart cried out, *Do you remember my name? I am looking for you. I need hope. I need you. I need confidence that you are nearby. I need a reason to keep going.*

I remember the next moment so vividly: I fell asleep, exhausted from all my striving. And I dreamt for the first time since the accident. In my dream, I was held by children—sweaty children in a home. I heard the most beautiful drums and music, and I saw dancing and the most colorful dresses. The sun felt warm as I looked out the window of this home and saw tremendous color. I felt alive for the first time in a long time. I actually pinched myself in the dream. I felt my hands reach up to touch my face and found a smile. I looked down at a little girl who was smiling back at me. I remember taking in deep breaths and feeling free from the chest-constricting heartache of the past few months. I slept soundly on the floor in my bungalow for the first time in such a long time.

Throughout the remaining days of spring and into summer, I went about my duties as a children's pastor and a spiritual director at our schools. I connected with the lives of kids and their families around me as we planned activities and events. There was more laughter, fewer tears, and more looking ahead, as I had a wedding to officiate on July 7, 2007. This commitment was a promise I had made before Terry died. Now I wasn't sure how I could perform such a ceremony. I was still reeling from the reality of "till death do us part." But this couple would not take no for an answer. They even played this card: "Terry and you agreed to this. You both prayed about it, and then you said 'yes.' Terry wouldn't want you to fall through on your word." These are the kind of friends I am so glad He has placed in my life; those who remind you of God's faithfulness through their own expressions of faith.

I boarded a plane to another continent to officiate a wedding at the seventh wonder of the world: Victoria Falls in Livingstone, Africa. My friends were worried. I was traveling alone, which concerned them. Do you know what excited me the most about this trip? I was going to be in the very city of one of missionaries I used to read and teach about before I was even ten years old: Dr. David Livingstone. I would be staying in the city of Zambia, where David's heart is buried (the rest

of his body is buried in Westminster Abbey). I would officiate the wedding atop Victoria Falls, named by Livingstone in
honor of Queen Victoria. How could I *not* go?

David Livingstone was a man born in Scotland who
became a missionary in Africa. Born in the early 1800s, he
was an explorer, abolitionist, and physician. He chose Africa
under the mantle of the London Missionary Society and,
during his time of service, discovered the cure for malaria and
encouraged people to visit and explore Africa. Some may consider him a failure at missionary work, since only one person
came to know Jesus personally, but no one doubted his love for
Africa and its people, culture, and possibilities.

Two of my favorite life-giving quotes from David Livingstone
are: "I am prepared to go anywhere, provided it be forward,"
and "If you have men who will only come if they know there is a
good road, I don't want them. I want men who will come if there
is no road at all." I'm drawn to these quotes for their clarity of
purpose and drive to find others who are like-minded.

God's presence was clearly felt on my twenty-four-hour
flight. People from all over the world were traveling to Africa
on missionary trips, safaris, or for humanitarian reasons.
I even met two groups that I later had the privilege to serve
alongside after the wedding, while the bride and groom
enjoyed their honeymoon. Apart from meeting others on the
plane, I had studying and sermon preparation to do. I would
preach for two weeks after I returned home from Africa.

The wedding was beautiful, and I was invigorated to spend

time where David Livingstone had lived and served. The most amazing moment on that trip for me was when my dream of the village children in the bright colors became a reality. I was invited to speak at a home where children lived after their parents died from AIDS. The home was run by local Christians and the greater church community. Right before I spoke, I was given an opportunity to pray with the local pastors in a separate room before entering the living room area full of kids.

I am a natural hugger when I meet people. One of the pastors was a large, muscular man who reminded me of Mr. T without the bling. I hugged him like I hug everyone I meet, and he pushed me away like I was a blazing hot griddle. I almost teared up as I looked at him. I was ready to apologize for offending him, but he wasn't interested in hearing me speak. In fact, he almost glared at me and asked loudly, "Do you not know the power that is in your hands?"

Trembling, I was unsure how to answer his question. I thought a simple "yes" or "no" would be wrong, so I placed my hands at my sides and looked at the ground and trembled.

He stepped closer, gripped my upper arms, and said, "Look at me." I looked at him immediately. Then he said, "Lift your hands up to me." I did as I was told. Then he held my hands very gently in his and asked quietly, "Do you not know that your hands are hands of healing?"

Again, tears streamed down my face. I answered, "To a degree—yes. I know that the Lord has me hold people in hugs until I feel their deep breath of letting go."

"That's healing," he said. "I felt it when you walked in and hugged me. Now there are kids in there who need to hear your invitation to Jesus and feel your touch of healing."

I gulped loudly then softly said, "I will go in now."

I was specifically asked to speak to the kids about the colors of my hair and of Jesus and His profound love for them. These were beautiful children who had been abandoned with no sense of belonging to a family or community. *Lord Jesus, what have I gotten myself into?* I prayed quietly. *How can I connect with them? Will you go before me? Make me not tremble in front of them.*

Into the living room I went. Mr. T followed me and stood at the door. I was guided to a chair in front of about one hundred kids whose ages ranged from birth to fifteen years old. They all sat on the floor. A single fan whirled above us in the room, which had to have had a temperature of at least one hundred degrees. I looked at the kids, smiled, and then glanced back to the door. The other two pastors smiled from ear to ear, and Mr. T crossed his arms over his huge chest. Sweat rolled down his bald head, arms, and through his shirt. He had no smile, but I saw the intensity in his eyes. I didn't fear him anymore; I only wondered what God had up His sleeve. I sensed more ahead.

I smiled at the kids and asked if they wanted to hear a story. Then I asked them about their favorite colors, and then it was my turn to smile. "Do you want hear my story?" I asked them. "It involves tons of colors." Here is what I told them:

"Yellow represents heaven, God's home, and His invitation for us to join him. Black represents our sin that separates us from God. Red represents God's love and the blood of His Son, Jesus, who paid for our sin to connect us to God. Brown represents the cross Jesus died on in our place. White represents our confession of our sins and acceptance of God's gift of salvation from our sin. Green represents God's desire for us to grow in Him—learning from His Word, living in accountable community, and serving Him. Purple represents our DNA; we are sons and daughters of the King Most High. Blue represents the reminder of Jesus' promise to return to gather up His family and live together forever. So go tell your friends! We can only decide on our eternity while living on this earth. Pink represents the call to love each person in front of us. We can't love as unconditionally as God does, but we should try. And orange represents the question, 'Orange you glad Jesus loves you?'"

After I had spoken for a few minutes, I asked the kids questions and listened to their responses.

"Do you understand that God loves you—each of you?" I asked.

"Yes!" they shouted in reply.

"Do you understand what sin is?"

"It's when I lie," one child said.

"It's when I steal food from the table," said another.

"It's when I don't love my brother or sister."

"It's when I feel angry with God for taking my mom and dad." This answer made many of us cry.

"Do you know that Jesus died for you? He took your place on the cross, so that God will see your sin paid for?"

"Yes, that's how much God loves me," they said, combined with my tears.

"Do you know that God knows you by name? Do you know that He speaks your name to you? Can you tell me your name?"

As name after name was shouted, the most amazing thing began to happen. From her seated position, a little girl walked toward me and repeated her name over and over. She sat facing me on my lap, and I realized all the kids were quiet as she spoke to me. I asked her how old she was and where she was from.

She told me her name was Blanca, and she was from South Africa. Her parents and animals were dead, but she had a sister in a crib here who was sick. She continued her story. She told me her family stole her house and moved her and her sick sister to this home. She then turned to the kids and told them to bow their heads because I had a question for them.

Uh, what? But suddenly, I knew the question: "Would you like to speak the name of Jesus and ask Him to come into your life?"

Usually when I ask that question, I take a deep breath and then ask if the individual would like to repeat a prayer after me. But this time, before I could finish my breath, the kids around the room started to say the name of Jesus powerfully and loudly. Blanca smiled and held onto my neck. She asked me to say her name into her ear so that she would know Jesus. I repeated "Blanca. Jesus loves Blanca. God loves Blanca."

"Jesus! Jesus! Jesus!" She repeated back.

I happened to look up and see Mr. T gesture toward two ladies to collect me while the other two pastors prayed powerfully over the seated children. Everyone began singing. I took Blanca's hand and walked to the back of the room where cribs and beds were filled with kids of every age. Also in those cribs were flies, smells, closed eyes, ashen faces, and skinny arms and legs. Loving staff members placed wet washcloths on their bodies and prayed aloud for them. It was quite a holy place. I didn't want to disturb anyone or anything as I sensed the presence of God. Mr. T directed me to a rocking chair and asked me to sit while they brought Blanca's sister to me. My head and spirit cried out inside of me: *And then what will I do? What is he expecting?* My heart turned to the God who brought me here, *What are you doing up there?*

I looked down at Blanca and asked, "Do you want to help me pray for your sister? We are going to ask God to help her, right?"

Blanca squeezed my hand, giggled, and helped me sit down on the rocker. She brought a little stool and placed it beside my chair. And then Mr. T brought in Blanca's sister. Oh. My. Heart. She was covered in sweat. Her tiny, dark brown ringlets were matted against her head. Her hands were oh so small. The nurse noticed my questioning gaze and told me Blanca's sister had had a fever for over three days. Then she looked at Blanca and said, "I think today is her last day, sweetie."

"No," Blanca said. "I know Jesus now. And He will let me talk to Him about her. Pastora Linda, what do now?"

I glanced quickly at Mr. T, the nurse, and Blanca, and then wrapped the thin, wet blanket around Blanca's baby sister. I put my right hand on her chest, and my left hand cradled her little head. I asked Blanca to hold her ankle. We were going to talk to Jesus, just like she said.

We began to pray—me, Blanca, the nurse, and Mr. T. We spoke different words in different languages, but the Lord heard and understood each of them. I picked up her little body and placed her on the left side of my chest, so that my neck could lean into her. Blanca held on. I suddenly felt as though someone poured a bucket of water over us. I was soaking wet. She had vomited and peed. The nurse saw the total confusion on my face and took Blanca's little sister. I wasn't sure if I should worry since I wore no medical gown or gloves and was now covered in bodily fluids from a child whose parents died of AIDS.

The nurse took the baby's temperature then started to smile and cry. She turned to Blanca and said, "Your sister won't die today. Jesus heard you. He knows your voice, Blanca. She doesn't have a temperature anymore. Blanca, she will live! Blanca, she will live."

I cried and locked eyes with Mr. T. Although no words were spoken, we rejoiced in the language of our hearts. And then, just as quickly, he turned to the nurse and said, "Bring her another. And don't stop until every child and nurse has been prayed over by Pastora and Blanca. God is about to do miracles today."

The next little baby they brought me was a little boy covered in sores that flies were feasting upon. He had hardly any eye movement and was limp in my arms. Blanca and I took our places. Again, I placed my right hand on his chest and cradled his head with my left hand. Blanca and I started to pray with our eyes wide open. His skin started to regenerate from the top of his head to the foot Blanca held—perfect, healthy skin. We didn't move an inch, but we smiled. We looked up at the nurse, pastors, and the other staff and kids who had gathered around us to witness this ongoing miracle. We prayed thanksgiving over and over again before the nurse took him from our hands.

Something else was happening too. It was weird at first; it seemed like flying shards of red glass were flashing in my mind's eye, first from the left and then from the right. Whatever it was looked like it was on a pedestal of some type. I had seen it first while holding Blanca's sister, but I just thought the heat and the powerful moment was getting to me. This afternoon was not what I had imagined when I said *yes* to speaking about Jesus and the colors of my hair. But this thing came back again after this little boy was healed. It was like a hand came down on my chest and rubbed a balm of sorts on my heart—the actual hope of healing within me.

Those thoughts didn't last long as another child was brought to us. Blanca knew each of them by name, and she told them that Jesus loved them and knew their name, and she prayed for them by name. We prayed for the remainder of the seventy-five kids and staff. Our prayers lasted the next two and a half hours, but we never saw another visible healing. My mind, however, kept seeing these flying shards start to resemble a vase—like a stained-glass piece that needed the leading in between to secure the pieces. I wish I could draw it for you, but you certainly didn't buy this book for my artistic renderings. By the end of the afternoon it was totally assembled.

Now that we had finished our prayers, Blanca and I went to the window where we heard music, laughter, drums, and singing ... my dream from earlier in the spring had come to life. This was the dream I had on my floor when the Lord put me to rest. I looked down, and there was Blanca: the same little girl who looked up at me months before in my dream. I pinched myself like I had done in my dream. And yes, on that day I saw the Lord perform miracles inside of and around me. Tears flowed unashamedly down my face as I realized my healing was finally beginning.

For the first time in close to a year, I actually felt that I was a vessel capable of holding water. I wouldn't just bleed out from the holes in my heart. Oh dear ones, you too can experience everything I have experienced. You can meet, know, and be known by Jesus. You can rest in the assurance that He has the best plan for you. You can know miracles—for you and perhaps even for others. You can know a life greater than you ever imagined. You will stand up again. You will walk again. The size of your steps doesn't matter. You can know restoration, renewal, and revival.

It will come. I wish I knew the date for you, but I don't. I am living proof that He is still at work through all the seasons of your life. What do you imagine? What fills your day, your dreams, and your visions? What fills your dreams at night and gives you hope? Don't let what you cannot do interfere with what you *can* do, and be willing to act on your dreams. If you don't imagine anything, then nothing ever happens.

Ask yourself, *Is what I'm doing today getting me closer to who I want to be, where I want to go, and what I want to accomplish and achieve?* If not, then stop. Reassess. And remember the first time you had that dream. Turn around and run toward it right now.

NEW PERSPECTIVES

1. Take moments to experience adventures within an adventure.
2. There are many ways to travel through our various seasons of struggles and challenges, but we all have different timetables for when we will stand again. Look at the changing of your seasons to give you hope. Don't compare your calendar with someone else's.
3. How have the roads you have traveled shaped you in your different seasons of life?
4. What have you seen, and how can you help someone who may be following you?
5. Do you need to rest and dream again?

12

Opening the Closet of Exchange

WE CAN'T PICK UP THE NEW UNTIL WE LAY DOWN THE OLD

You have turned my mourning into joyful
dancing. You have taken away my clothes of
mourning and clothed me with joy.

PSALM 30:11

*H*ave you ever wanted something that belonged to someone else? Have you maybe even wished to live someone else's life? Even though we romanticize these types of exchanges, they're not always as wonderful as we may have imagined.

Twenty months after Terry's death, I was boarding a plane to visit my friends' home in Mexico. I planned to stay for a couple of weeks. I only knew a few people in the housing development where their home was located, but I knew this time away would be great. I imagined waking up in the morning, spending time with Jesus in His Word, cooking breakfast, and then making the biggest decision of the day: Which bathing suit would I wear all day? I would enjoy my days reading at the beach or the pool. Around mid-afternoon, I would shower, take a nap, and then cook dinner before watching movies into the evening. Of course, I would also cry between the hours, but I would check in with different people every day, so that no one would be afraid something may have happened to me.

As I boarded the plane and took my seat, a picture flashed in front of me. It looked like an old-fashioned wardrobe—much like the tall wardrobe in C. S. Lewis' book *The Lion, The Witch and the Wardrobe.* The picture started moving; the doors to the wardrobe opened, and hanging in the closet was a single dress on a hanger. The dress was familiar to me; it was the Easter dress my grandmother had made for me when I was five or six years old. I smiled at this memory because it brought me such joy. I had felt so beautiful wearing it as a child. The picture was gone as quickly as it had appeared.

The picture wandered in and out of my consciousness—so much so, that I actually looked for the wardrobe in each of the rooms of my friends' home. But there was no wardrobe like the one I had seen on the plane days before. After ten days in their home, I came inside from an afternoon in the warm sun and decided to take a nap before showering. I laid down on my bed and quickly went to sleep. When I awakened, I sat on the foot of the bed and reached for my clothes from the little area where I had been storing them. But now in that area was the wardrobe once again, and it seemed so real!

The wardrobe door opened before me. Sure enough, my childhood Easter dress hung inside. The top part of the dress dropped to my hips and was light pink, and yellow piping separated the top from the dark burgundy skirt. My grandma could sew! I remember twirling in that dress; it took flight every time I wore it.

Then came another surprise. I could see my grandmother sitting on her couch with me years later with *my* dress in her hands.

"Honey, we must put this dress away and save it for your cousins for when they get older," my grandmother said.

"But why, Grandma?" I asked. "You made this for me. It's mine."

"Honey, it doesn't fit you anymore," she reassured me. "You have taken such good care of it. We can give it to your younger cousin. Wouldn't it be wonderful to share this dress together?"

"No, Grandma. It would *not* be wonderful. It's mine."

"Linda, you can no longer wear this, so let's save it and keep the memory alive. You can share all the fun you had in this dress with her, and she'll share her new adventures with you."

"No. No. No, Grandma!" I stomped my feet. Thinking I had to come up with a clever reason to keep my dress, I paused to think. Then I had an idea. I said, "Grandma, can't we just put it away and save it for *my* little girl to wear? Wouldn't that be wonderful? A part of you continues."

And just as easy as it is for you to read how selfish I was acting, I too realized just how self-centered I was in that moment on the bed. I stopped in the stillness of that conversation, and tears began to fall. I found myself apologizing to God for the ugliness I saw in myself.

I looked up to see another garment hanging next to the Easter dress. It was my college graduation gown. My graduation day was wonderful! The weather could not have been more perfect. Only a few, white, wispy clouds floated overhead. The temperature was in the mid-seventies, and my family was in attendance. They sat on chairs on a big lawn, and I felt so excited as I stood in line with my friends, ready to walk in the processional.

As exciting as reliving all those moments and emotions were, I found myself anticipating the conversation that would be coming. But there was no conversation, just thoughts:

Linda, I am so proud of you.

You are the first in our family to attend and graduate from college.

You are setting expectations high for yourself and our family.

I looked around. I was looking for the faces of those family members who were speaking to me on that day. I couldn't find any. But I did look inside and asked out loud, "Lord, what is it that you want me to see or hear?"

Silence.

And then in the silence, I heard the Lord in my spirit and in the depths of my soul: *Always set the goal before you to stay in a place of wanting to learn. Remain a forever learner … a disciple of me. Accomplishments like your graduation are a gift from me. Keep moving forward. I will be with you.*

My head dropped in respect of the One who was talking to me. I looked toward the wardrobe where another garment was now hanging. I burst into tears—really ugly tears. The kind of tears that take your breath away. I began to sob uncontrollably as my second glance at the wardrobe confirmed what I had already seen: my wedding dress. "Oh, no," I wailed. "You are breaking my heart here, Lord. What can you possibly want to say to me about the greatest day of my life?"

I cried in that room for a long time—waves and waves of heavy sobs, quiet tears, and rocking myself back and forth on the edge of that bed. My alarm went off, and the noise startled me. I must have been in there for a long time if I was still awake when my alarm went off. I had set it as a reminder to wake up an hour before sunset. I never wanted to miss those, but time had seemed to stop altogether that night.

I remembered our engagement. I remembered planning our wedding day, when we took a trip to the courthouse and then loaded the boxes from my apartment and the boxes from his apartment into a rented truck and left Southern California for Northern California adventures. Some things were sure, and other things were not so sure. But we had each other, and we knew God was sending us.

It was an adventure for two. And the adventures continued until they suddenly ended. Grief rolled over me afresh. Sobs escaped as I cried, "What can I do now, Lord? It's been twenty months, and my heart *still* hurts! Why can't I ever heal? When will I ever get better? I am still waiting. And certainly, my friends and family are waiting too."

As I continued to look at the dress and experience moments from when I had worn it, I realized I had never taken my eyes off of that dress. Something inside of me did not want to lose all of this again. I felt like I could take that dress off the hanger and hold it forever. I could put it on and twirl myself back in time, so that these past twenty months had never happened.

It was time for me to stop living in the past. Although I didn't *want* to stop living in the past, deep inside I knew I would need to if I was going to survive. I wanted to live … I just didn't know how.

"Lord, I need you to teach me how to do this," I prayed. "I can't keep wanting to be back in the past; help me want to be present."

I wasn't afraid of the adventure. I wasn't even afraid of doing it alone. I just didn't know where to start. I knew this moment was going to be life-changing, and I asked Him, "Lord, what now?" I lowered my gaze from the wardrobe that held my wedding dress and other precious garments, and I waited in silence. Tremendous peace came over me. I felt a presence in the room and a weight lift from my shoulders.

I cannot describe the lump in my throat that gradually

disappeared or how my breath began to slow down, but I was not ready for the thoughts the Lord delivered to me next. I immediately felt the urge to look again into the wardrobe. Next to my wedding dress was an empty hanger. Then the words came: *My dear Linda, please remove your sweater of grief and place it on the hanger.*

I felt like I was back to where I started with the Easter dress my grandmother had made for me. I felt betrayed, annoyed, and ready to fight! "No, Lord," I said. "I can't take this off! Who will I be? I thought you said I wouldn't have to forget? I thought I was doing this 'grief' life as you wanted? Lord, I don't think I can give up one more thing." Then I said, "I am not strong enough. ... Do I have to?"

Then the promises from God's Word came flooding back into my heart and mind:

- He would change my mourning into dancing. (Psalm 30:11)
- He would change my ashes into a new crown of beauty. (Isaiah 61:3)
- He would change my weakness into strength. (Joel 3:10)
- He would wipe away all my tears. (Revelation 21:4)
- He would be the God of all comfort. (1 Corinthians 1:3–5)
- He would be near the brokenhearted and the crushed in spirit. (Psalm 34:18)

- And the verse that carried me often during these times: "I love the LORD because he hears my voice and my prayers for mercy. Because he bends down to listen, I will pray as long as I have breath!" (Psalm 116:1–2)

I asked quietly, "Will I have to forget? Because this sweater of grief seems to be all that I have. I have learned how to walk alone as a widow, even in the presence of friends and family, and yet I have seen you grow me and make me courageous and confident. These will still be new waters I have to learn to tread. I don't know if I can do this. I trust you, Lord—you have led me this far—but I don't think I can trust if I have to forget."

And with the tenderness only our heavenly Father can bring us, I felt He heard me cry out to Him. And here is what I heard; *My dear daughter, Linda. I have seen and felt every one of your tears of anguish and despair. I have never closed my eyes or ears to your struggle. But it's time to dance again. It's time to be hopeful again. And if you would, remember that I have always been faithful to every one of my promises.*

Look in the wardrobe again. I promise you today that I will always be giving you a new wardrobe—hangers filled with adventures. I promise you. There may be a time you will need to put these "old" clothes on to show others that I provide new clothes. I don't want you to ever feel the weight or sting of remembering these different seasons in your life; I have designed each of them for you.

On that day, I hung up my sweater of grief. I have put each of these garments on again at times throughout the years—most recently to write this chapter for you. But I want to encourage you to take Him at His Word when you look into the wardrobe of your life. Perhaps today will be the day you can see the new hangers with new designer clothes just for you!

NEW PERSPECTIVES

1. What's hanging in your closet that represents the seasons of your life?
2. Are there any old garments (addiction, grief, anger, etc.) that you keep putting back on even though you know you need to remove them?
3. What new designer garments has the Lord made for you (confidence, compassion, joy, etc.)? Is the story ready to be told to someone else today?
4. Take a moment and look at the wardrobe of your life and express your gratitude to God.

13

Be a Person of Impact and Influence

YOU ARE A CHANGE-MAKER

If you can't feed a hundred people,
than feed just one.

MOTHER TERESA

*I*f I saw the words of this chapter title, I would want to read the whole thing. But if I then read the words in the subtitle, I would doubt myself, or think *I can't be that person. I am just a little lady who is four-foot-ten with size three feet and very colorful hair. I can certainly attract people, but can I impact them?*

The truth is that we can all impact and influence others every day of our lives. Have you ever heard it said, "A good attitude is contagious?" Grumpy, critical attitudes can be contagious too. You see, every day we influence others and they influence us. I am especially drawn to strong people of character and integrity. I like movies that display strength during times of uncertainty in the plot. I like heroes! I like women who are warriors who protect others. I like to be surprised by a person who finds his or her voice and uses it!

But I haven't always viewed myself that way. I always had tall friends and thought I would be able to see all the world if I was tall too. I had the lower and shorter perspective, while tall people had the higher perspective. I didn't grow up thinking I was pretty enough or good enough to be liked. I was funny, but not like the popular girls. I was picked first to play kickball since I practiced, so I was good enough, but I was not the first person picked to go to the movies with a group of people. I learned early to rotate my clothes in the closet to make it appear as though I had lots of clothes, but in truth I was creatively matching different blouses with different skirts and slacks. And on the funnier side, I was never picked first to play on a team of tetherball, basketball, or volleyball, but I did learn skills that made me a viable teammate in middle school, like being a great free-throw shooter in basketball or serving well in volleyball.

I was motivated to learn whatever I needed to learn or practice whatever I needed to practice, so that I would be picked for an activity. I am not quite sure where I learned that, but I think it began to teach me that much of my life was within my power to change, as long as I had the desire to do so. My greatest desire was to be seen—being short sometimes has the opposite effect (at least at first). I learned from my mom and grandmother that bad behavior would garner attention, but not in a way that was acceptable in our household. So *that* wasn't an option.

I became a great student at school. I always sat in the front row of the classroom so that I could at least see the teacher or the whiteboard. I loved school, and I really enjoyed learning. My desire to learn overflowed into my spiritual life too. When I learned that the word *disciple* meant to be a "learner," I decided in third grade that I would be a "forever learner and disciple" of Jesus. I was an overachiever when it came to learning my Scripture verses for Sunday school every week. I read God's Word every day. More than anything, I wanted to be a person of impact and influence who brought people to meet Jesus. I wanted to be a warrior! I wanted Jesus to see *and* hear me. I wanted Him to see something in me that had value.

I expected my do-whatever-you-can-to-be-chosen approach to the rest of my life to extend into my spiritual life. I was surprised there weren't a ton of hoops to jump through or tasks to master to be worthy enough for Jesus. I knew I wasn't worthy enough on my own, but I knew that He found me worthy enough to love and die for. I just wanted Jesus to pick me!

When I became a widow, I searched the Scriptures—looking for God, for guidelines, navigation tools, and wanting to be seen by God again. All those feelings of not being good enough rose to the surface of my consciousness. After all, it had been wonderful to be seen by Mr. Wonderful each morning as we awakened, talked about our love for each other, and walked through victories and challenges together. But now I was alone, and I missed sharing life with him. I missed being his "one and only," as he said to me daily. And now, no longer being half of a couple, I came to God with all my victories and challenges.

During my trip to Africa, I had begun to prepare to preach at our church in late July. I was going to preach from Luke 13:10–13 about the woman who was hunched over. I want you to read the passage first, and then I'll share some of how the Lord impacted and influenced me as I applied this story to my own life. This is not a deep, theological study; it's simply my perspective of a woman and how Jesus viewed her. My desire is that as we look at this together, you will be impacted and influenced by the God who sees you.

> On a Sabbath Jesus was teaching in one of the synagogues, and a woman was there who had been crippled by a spirit for eighteen years. She was bent over and could not straighten up at all. When Jesus saw her, he called her forward and said to her, "Woman, you are set free from your infirmity." Then he put his hands on her, and immediately she straightened up and praised God. (NIV)

The Lord was teaching in one of the synagogues when He

saw a woman there. Now in the days of Jesus, the women were not allowed in the synagogues near the men. They had their own area separated by a divider. However, I can't help but think that because she had been hunched over for eighteen years, she was somewhat invisible to others regardless of where she was. Her hunch was from something not yet diagnosed.

She must have felt like an outcast. Something literally crippled her, so that her only vision was that of her dusty feet. She was always looking down. How difficult it would have been for her to hear all of life around her and not be able to lift her head or even participate with others. Perhaps, with each passing day and year, she became more and more withdrawn. It's likely she wasn't invited to events with family and friends.

Have you ever felt like this? Have you ever felt withdrawn because of your choices or circumstances? Perhaps, you have felt isolated as well. Whatever it was that changed her posture—be it medically, psychologically, spiritually, or even emotionally—it stayed with her for eighteen years. She couldn't explain the "why" behind this posture. In fact, no one could.

For many of my early days as a widow, I felt like I was only eating dirt or dust; food had no substance or flavor. It felt like my body was getting older by the day. I didn't have the energy much less the inclination to participate in much of anything, let alone social engagements. I had no breath in my lungs. I kept looking down and working. Simple tasks I had done before seemed to take a long time for me to perform, and my life felt like it collected more and more dreariness and dust.

You see, I *was* this hunched woman. I was the woman who I was preparing to preach about. I could barely gather the energy to read the rest of the passage, and yet I wanted to read it because there was hope that maybe I could learn how to navigate these waters. And then, there it was in the next verse: Jesus saw her! In the middle of His teaching, the Bible says that He saw her!

I'm guessing she didn't notice that He saw her because her vision was cast downward. And maybe He saw her because she was in a place she should not have been. Whatever the case, the point is that He saw her exactly where she was, and He knew she had a condition that made her look down.

I know where she was at emotionally; I was in the same place. Maybe you are too. Even though her story is amazing, let's look at what Jesus did next. He saw her, and then He called her forward. Do you get each of those words?

He: Jesus.

Called: What tone do you think He used when He called her? How did He address her? What did He call her?

Her: She was the only woman in the room. How do you think she felt? Embarrassed? Did she even know who was calling her? I am guessing she did because He was teaching, and she would have known His voice. Did He stop in the middle of His teaching to call to her or did he approach her after the fact?

Forward: This word is powerful to me. It shows movement. She couldn't stay where she was in the shadows as an invisible woman in a male-dominated room. He was calling her to move toward Him. And it showed direction, just like when God calls us forward. Leave your stuff behind; drop it on the floor and come forward! The Lord desires progress for us. He desires more for us. And this may have been a whole new path for her—maybe one she hadn't traveled before.

The hunched woman's story got me thinking a little differently. It was as if God was saying to me, *Step out, Linda. Come forward to me. I have more for you. I know it's unfamiliar but come toward my voice.*

The next part of this narrative is just as thrilling and life-giving to each of us. He said to her, "Woman, you are set free from your infirmity." How many of us need to hear those words? You are set free from your infirmity. What holds you in bondage? What holds you in captivity? What invisible chains need to drop to the floor? In this passage, the Lord set her free from her infirmity—that physical weakness or disease that rendered her hunched over for eighteen years, but I believe the Lord was speaking with even greater authority—deeper into her soul, just like He does for us.

As I mentioned earlier, I was this woman: I was hunched over in my grief. My vision became more focused on the ground, so much so that I stopped looking up. When I met with the Lord in the early mornings, I seemed to always greet Him with my head, heart, and spirit downcast. I loved climbing onto His lap and Him holding me as I cried.

As I write this book, I am again in the throes of cancer—the diagnosis, treatment, and side effects—and in such need for the Lord to "set me free from *this* infirmity" and the infirmity of my heart—discouraged, desperate for Jesus, and growing too tired and fatigued to even *want* to keep fighting.

In fact, I am this woman—again! I don't understand the "why" behind this cancer diagnosis: a diagnosis that began in my early twenties when I had to come home from the mission field and remain stateside. These were not the plans for my life, nor did I think it was where the Lord had led or called me. But this cancer has returned multiple times. Multiple body parts have been surgically removed with the lasting consequence of never being able to birth children.

But it's not always the external that needs setting free. Sometimes we need healing on the inside, where pain can feel even more disabling. My heart is discouraged again, but I try—with labored breath—to choose joy. To choose life.

It is always an act of faith in my God to trust Him. It may not be evident. It may not ever be truly understood. But I can say that He is faithful. His Word and every promise is true ... even to me, this woman who is so much like the woman of Luke 13.

Perhaps you are struggling today—with one thing, or perhaps with many things. Jesus says to you today, "Woman (or man), you are set free!" This is said in the present tense. Jesus says that today, right now, you are set free from your infirmity. Claim it. Proclaim it. And do it today.

After Jesus declared in Luke 13 that she was healed, He

placed His hands on her and immediately she straightened up and praised God. Such wonderfulness right there! He didn't put just one hand on her but both hands. He was totally engaged. I am not sure if He placed His hands on her head, her shoulders, or if He reached down and touched her hands, but He was not put off by her infirmity.

Jesus knew the power in His hands, and He wanted to give it to her so she could be made well. He wants to give it you and to me. Oh, that we would know and experience the power of His hands on us and our lives. And you know what? She didn't even have to ask for it! He gave it willingly. I wonder how many blessings of His touch I have not experienced because I wasn't nearby for Him to reach out to me.

Her response to His touch was immediate. The same happens to us! The cancer may not be gone right now, or the consequences from our decisions may not have yet ceased, but with His touch that woman straightened up. With His touch, we are changed!

Those are bold words for us. Maybe *we* just need to straighten up. Maybe we just need to change our sights from looking down to looking up: up to His Word, up to His eyes, up and away from whatever causes us to look down, and up and away from the baggage that weighs us down. Not only did the hunched woman see Jesus, but she also praised God. She knew who rescued her from herself. She knew who the power came from. She was standing next to the very Son of God who saw her, called her, set her free, and then touched her. That was when everything changed.

I believe every word of God in the Bible are words we can claim. I believe God picked out the very events He wanted us to hear and see. I believe I can claim this in my life. How about you? Let's consider what we can take away from this Bible passage and how can we apply it to our lives:

- You are *not* invisible to God—no matter where you are, or how long you have been there, or how heavy a load you may carry, or how bent-over you may feel.
- Jesus *sees* you.
- Jesus calls you *forward*.
- Jesus says that you are set *free*.
- His touch is one of *healing*.

The hunched woman straightened up immediately and praised God. This same story can be yours today. This can be my story again too. Get ready to tell your story.

I would like to encourage you to listen to "The Reckless Love of God," as it's a song that I sing many times a day. The song speaks of the overwhelming, never-ending, reckless love of God. Sometimes in my despair of this recent health challenge, it has been good for me to remember how much Jesus loves me and the lengths He will go to for me and for you.

NEW PERSPECTIVES

1. Conduct an inventory of friends and family who influence you. Pursue relationships with those who inspire you to be the best version of yourself, as God intended.
2. Are there things in your life that you need to get off your shoulders—things that cause you to be "hunched over" and keep you from enjoying life around you?
3. Claim a new perspective to see what God has intended for you today.
4. Spend some quiet time reflecting on "The Reckless Love of God" and thanking God for His desire for you. Then live today consciously aware of His love.

EPILOGUE

The Adventure Continues

Well, let's just say my life has been quite an adventure. Not that I would necessarily choose all of the adventures that I've had, but I have seen the value of each of them. I realize that adventures are the best way to learn. So whenever possible, choose adventure. Take the risk! In the end, we will only regret the adventures we did not take.

I have seen lots of cement, met lots of people, taken many detours, endured rough roads, enjoyed the warmth of the sun, laughter, new sights, and the smells of nature. The food, however, was always good; I never had a bad meal. Our senses seem heightened when we put away our busyness and concentrate on our present.

Remember the quote from Helen Keller that I shared with you earlier: "Life is either a daring adventure or nothing at all." Harsh words! Yet no truer words have ever been spoken! Go for it! Life begins at the end of your comfort zone. Go climb your mountains. Collect those precious moments—not the material things that won't last!

So much has happened since Africa. The Lord has called

me back to serve in my own backyard in Northern California as a children's pastor and then a full-time missionary at Praying Pelican Missions. By the time this book is printed, I will have been with Praying Pelican Missions for five years, and Mr. Wonderful has been home with Jesus for twelve years. I have been on tons of planned missionary trips and tons of everyday, ordinary missionary adventures.

Since that time, I met (and married) Mr. Romance. He is a Frank Sinatra entertainer and has been wowing audiences for over forty years. He brought to our marriage the children I never got to bear: three children and one grandchild. He loves Jesus, and he loves me. He sings to me and dances with me in the very kitchen where I screamed at God to bring the music back into my life. But that's another story ... or maybe another book.

Being an adventurer brings adventures. I have more to live out and to tell, just as you do. I want you to know, most of all, that God has a plan for my life, and He has a plan for yours as well. God not only has a plan, but He also loves you deeply. Unconditionally. Forever. There are no hoops for you to jump through to earn His love. There is no sin, decision, or addiction that is too big for His abundant grace and mercy toward you. He shows up in our everyday, ordinary lives.

You don't need to be a pastor or a missionary. You don't need to be four-foot-ten with size three feet and colorful hair. He made you as a masterpiece that no one can duplicate: there is only one of you. You are amazing. Turn your life around. It's in you. It's possible for you! You can make the choice today. In fact, each of your experiences makes you a person of impact and influence. You have a story to tell, so go tell it.

And now, before we end this adventure together, I wanted to leave you with one last picture. I wanted to leave this here for those who may want to look to the back of the book to figure out what happens in the story. I'm grateful to my godson, Cameron, who took this picture because it has significance.

My late husband's great friend, George, purchased this Harley because he wanted to keep it in the family. Yep, this bike that I am sitting on is the very bike that Terry and I had so many adventures on. It's the very bike he was riding when his life ended. Oh. My. Goodness. It was hard to climb back on this Harley. My legs weren't even sure how to do it. George said to me, "Go ahead. Your body will remember."

The problem was that my heart already remembered, but I chose to be brave for you. I wanted you to know that you can step up to anything that scares or hurts you, and you can win. You can choose to turn your life around. Believe me when I say you can. You made me brave before I ever knew you.

Acknowledgments

I am so grateful to the Lord who gave me the words to write.

I am so thankful for Mr. Romance, Jesse Castillo, who gave me encouragement, prayers, love, and corrections in red ink. He stood with me in laughter, tears, discouragement, and despair. He continues to love me with his whole heart, and I am thankful for the adventurer he is as he serves his Lord.

With appreciation, I know that this book would never have been written if it had not been for the many women who have stood with me over the years. These fierce warriors are the ones who made me who I am today. Thank you "Aunt Jo" L, Linda W, Rachel Z, Stacey H, Connie R, Terri W, Mary G, Therese T, Kathryn F, Eli A, Carolyn W, JoAnne C, Debbie T, Fane M, Joanie E, Sandi P, Joanne B, Michele M, Jodi J, and Karon H. So many women have come alongside me and to name them all, I'd fill this book and another one. I am humbled, and I am grateful.

In gratitude, I must speak of the men who have taught me, mentored me, encouraged me, prayed over and into me, and set my heart aflame for the Lord's calling on my life. I am thankful to have served with many of them in leadership, and I am forever appreciative for their influence and impact on my life. Thank you "Uncle Malcolm" L, Pastor Hous, Pastor Dave F, Pastor Joe J, Pastor Mike B, Pastor Samuel B, Pastor Stan F, Pastor Tim R, Matt P, Bill W, Frank H, Dave W, Marcus T, and George C.

And although they can't read, I am thankful for the unconditional love of my kitties, Oreo and Little Man. They sat by the heater or laid in the sun while I wrote. They purred as they sat on the printer as the hard copy printed. Silly, maybe, but I am definitely thankful.

Thank you, BroadStreet Publishing, for setting me on a course and seeing me to the end. It hasn't all been easy (tons and tons of tears), but you have certainly been used by God in my life to write and write and write. May God bless these words in the heart of each reader.

About the Author

A teacher, pastor, missionary, storyteller, and adventurer, LINDA VANNOY-CASTILLO is passionate about glorifying God and helping people find purpose in Him. She's a San Francisco Bay Area native who enjoys sporting colorful hair and riding motorcycles. Linda currently serves as the director of ministry at Praying Pelican Missions. Learn more about Linda and her adventures at castilloadventures.com.